TEACHER
ROUNDS

for Mark J. Hopkins, great friend and teacher

and

for the dedicated partner school principals
and teachers of Main South

3860 La Reunion Pkwy.
Dallas, TX 75212
servicedfw@hpb.com

Items:

Qty	Title	Locator	Condition
1	Teacher Rounds: A Guide to Collaborative Learning in and...	BSD-1-1-020-001-1702	Good

Subtotal:
Shipping:
Total:

Marketplace:	AmazonMarketplaceUS
Order Number:	4415969
Ship Method:	Standard
Customer Name:	Wyatt Lewis
Order Date:	8/30/2019 5:47:13 AM
Marketplace Order #:	111-0347646-7266621
Email:	696wp51q0342d8q@marketplace.amazon.com

Thanks for your Order!

If you have any questions or concerns regarding this order, please contact us at servicedfw@hpb.com

TEACHER ROUNDS

A Guide to Collaborative Learning in and From Practice

Thomas Del Prete

CORWIN
A SAGE Company

CORWIN
A SAGE Company

FOR INFORMATION:

Corwin

A SAGE Company

2455 Teller Road

Thousand Oaks, California 91320

(800) 233-9936

www.corwin.com

SAGE Publications Ltd.

1 Oliver's Yard

55 City Road

London EC1Y 1SP

United Kingdom

SAGE Publications India Pvt. Ltd.

B 1/I 1 Mohan Cooperative Industrial Area

Mathura Road, New Delhi 110 044

India

SAGE Publications Asia-Pacific Pte. Ltd.

3 Church Street

#10-04 Samsung Hub

Singapore 049483

Acquisitions Editor: Dan Alpert

Associate Editor: Kimberly Greenberg

Editorial Assistant: Heidi Arndt

Production Editor: Brittany Bauhaus

Copy Editor: Michelle Ponce

Typesetter: C&M Digitals (P) Ltd.

Proofreader: Laura Webb

Indexer: Rick Hurd

Cover and Graphic Designer: Janet Kiesel

Permissions Editor: Karen Ehrmann

Copyright © 2013 by Corwin

Printed in the United States of America

Library of Congress Cataloging-in-Publication Data

A catalog record of this book is available from the Library of Congress.

9781452268156

This book is printed on acid-free paper.

SUSTAINABLE FORESTRY INITIATIVE

Certified Chain of Custody
Promoting Sustainable Forestry
www.sfiprogram.org
SFI-01268

SFI label applies to text stock

13 14 15 16 17 10 9 8 7 6 5 4 3 2 1

Contents

Figures

Preface

The professional world of teachers is beset by a storm of seemingly conflicting forces. On the one hand, teachers are urged to reflect, to collaborate, and to build strong professional learning communities. There is, in fact, ample testimony of the power of teacher collaboration for enhancing the professional well-being and practice of teachers (see, for example, Carroll, Fulton, and Doerr, June 2010; Darling-Hammond and Bransford, 2005; Fullan, 2007; McLaughlin and Talbert, 2001; Troen and Boles, 2012). There is strong evidence as well that students benefit when their teachers work together reflectively in a culture of mutual support and trust (Bryk and Schneider, 2002). But this theme in teachers' work exists in disheartening tension with the rising system of prescribed and controlled curricula and its pressing demand for testable and measurable results, with teachers, just as their students are, increasingly subjected to narrowly conceived evaluation schemes in the name of accountability.

This is not to suggest that curricular rigor and student performance are questionable academic priorities or that there is no need for accountability—far from it. But when they become monolithic concerns, as they are in the lives of so many public school teachers, they diminish if not exclude other enriching and, arguably, essential factors in learning. They funnel the lives of teachers and their students into narrowing channels of work and possibility. They encourage institution centeredness rather than person centeredness: they feed bureaucracy rather than personal commitment, integrity, and community. At their worst, they impose a simplistic corporate ideal of efficiency, production, and evaluation on what is a complex human and cultural endeavor influenced by an array of factors, not least whether students have healthy and stable personal lives. Even when more nuanced, the solutions of the day tend to reduce the idea of education to what is quantifiable rather than to align it with what is desirable in terms of capabilities of mind, character (or "heart"), and participation in our democratic civic culture.

It is important for a book that aspires to make a contribution to the practice of teaching to start by stating where it stands with respect to the current climate. As much as we might do better in developing schools and communities that live up to ideals of equity and opportunity for all students, I question, along with many of my colleagues, whether education in any meaningful sense will be improved with greater measurement of teachers and students as the driving theory of change. There is another path, one that strives to honor our democratic values and the teaching profession, that strives to tap our deepest human capacities, and that treats all students as if they were our own children. On this path, we keep in view our core purpose to develop the mind, character, and civic responsibility of each student and a core belief that each is capable and worthy beyond our ken. We strive to create a space—a culture—in which we can live and work honestly, respectfully, reflectively, and inquiringly, individually and together, according to our fullest vocational aspiration. We learn to guide and sustain each other. We show accountability by taking coresponsibility. Instead of focusing first of all on effectiveness and results, we concentrate our practice on knowing and serving each student here and now as a growing thinker, reader, writer, speaker, and responsible actor. Faced with the inherent complexity of this task, particularly in distressed locations, we strive for shared insight and understanding, the mutual development of capable practice and expertise, and collaborative action. Out of our commitment, mutual respect, mutual support, and integrity we strive to make an educational community, one as strong in its warm regard for and ability to draw out all that is best and possible in students as in its sense of educational purpose.

Teachers need learning practices which uphold the integrity of teaching—which respect and honor its challenge and responsibility. They need practices that can be applied in their own classroom, school, and partnership contexts, practices they can call their own. In the midst of a culture saturated with quantitative information, they need practices that focus on the personal and qualitative: practices through which they act and think as professionals who care about, regularly examine, and think through their complex work deeply, practices which also help them to form a true learning community. This book introduces one practice—Teacher Rounds—meant to support collaborative learning centered on student learning and the practice that fosters it. It suggests the value, for students as well as for teachers, of a culture in which teachers learn together, in their own classrooms, to develop insight, capable practice, and expertise, as compared to a culture driven by reductive notions of effectiveness and results.

A Teacher Round

A group of five secondary teachers, including one preservice teacher, commandeer a table in a cramped basement space that doubles as a meeting place and cafeteria. One teacher provides a handout and soon after begins to explain goals and challenges that he or she is addressing in an upcoming class. It is a customary scene at the school—the prelude to a Teacher Round. Teacher Rounds have long been a core professional learning practice for the teachers, a way to bring theory, practice, context, and expertise dynamically together.

The teacher who begins is the host teacher for the Round. He or she passes out copies of a Round Sheet to members of the group, who read it silently. The host teacher then reviews key aspects of what is on the sheet:

- a background section that sets the curricular, academic, and social context of the learning and teaching that the group will observe;
- a learning focus section that describes the focus of student and teacher learning; and, critically,
- a "round inquiry" that asks for evidence relevant to understanding the learning and teaching.

Members of the Round group intermittently ask for clarification or elaboration or try to bring assumptions and details more fully to light. The host Round teacher indicates whether group members will observe or interact in some specified way with students once the class (the actual Round) is underway. After about 15 to 20 minutes, the preround discussion is complete, and the Round group moves upstairs and enters a classroom. Each member takes up a different observational post in a chair alongside a group of three students. The Round begins and the next hour or so is spent in close observation or interaction with students and in note taking.

When the class ends, the Teacher Round group reconvenes in an empty classroom (the teacher meeting room or hallway are alternatives). The postround discussion starts. The host teacher shares his or her initial thoughts about what happened relative to the focus of learning and his or her expectations and goals. Attention then turns to the questions the host teacher formulated to frame the Round inquiry. Different members of the Round group offer observations corresponding to the first of the Round questions; they take each question in turn, with particular observations sometimes leading to a more general reflection on practice based on the learning or teacher action in question. Group members compare notes on the engagement and learning of individual learners. They discuss various aspects of the designed learning process in relation to the actual dynamic of learning. The host Round teacher concludes with his or her takeaways and ponderings and implications for the next day's teaching. Then, Round participants give the host teacher their written notes corresponding to the Round questions. After 20 minutes or so the group breaks up.

In broad outline this is a Teacher Round as practiced in partner schools with Clark University and in other schools adopting the practice; Teacher Rounds are also woven into the Master of Arts in Teaching program at the University (Del Prete, 1997 & 2010). A Teacher Round is a classroom-based collaborative learning practice shaped primarily by and for teachers to learn in, about, and from practice. It follows a simple protocol but calls into play a range of professional dispositions and skills, in particular observation, reflection, inquiry, and collaborative discussion. Also, as much as it may have value in and of itself, a Teacher Round usually does not stand alone; it typically integrates into a more involved learning process. The Teacher Round described above, for example, is an actual on-the-ground, in-practice segment of an ongoing conversation about teaching and learning in teacher teams. If the Round had been conducted by a teacher preparation student, then he or she might follow up by reviewing video footage of the Round, possibly with peers in a practice workshop, and writing a postround reflection. Even in this more extended process, however, the Round—classroom-based and teacher-framed—is the primer or touchstone, the place where idea, action, context, reflection, and reflective friends intertwine, where, to use the vernacular, the rubber hits the road.

Teacher Rounds, the Medical Model, and Practice-Based Education

Rounds are a staple practice in medical education. Yet, although educators such as Shulman (2004) have looked at the medical model to inform teacher education and practice, Rounds have not been translated widely into a comparable practice in teacher learning. A version of Rounds was introduced in two different professional development school start-ups in Massachusetts in the late 1980s. The Clark version derives from one of them (Del Prete, 1990). Others, some drawing on the Clark model, have introduced Teacher Rounds in their teacher preservice programs (see Appendix B).

Recently, Harvard educators have developed a model of instructional rounds designed to understand a school's or school system's instructional practice through the eyes of a team of observers (City, Elmore, Fiarman, and Teitel, 2009). But instructional rounds are fundamentally different from the more collaborative and highly contextualized—indeed, more personal and intimate—Teacher Round model presented in this book. Instructional rounds are conducted by a team of educators, drawn from networks with a common interest in improving instruction at a systemic scale, who visit classrooms within a particular school at a point in time in order to gather and share classroom-based observations relevant to a problem of practice that the school or a district is trying to address. A Teacher Round, in contrast, is led by a teacher in her or his classroom; it is conducted mainly by, for, and with teachers as a reflective, inquiring, and collaborative learning process. Whereas instructional rounds glean broad characteristics of practice in a school, a Teacher Round strives to understand teaching and learning in detail and depth, in context, so that participants might better understand and develop their own practice. At the same time, the two models of rounds have an important similarity and complementarity. They overlap in particular to the extent that they are practices dedicated to understanding teaching and learning by making the practice inside classrooms more open, visible, and understandable.

The Teacher Round model, as in the case of instructional rounds, draws from the medical model. It aims similarly to uncover practice—to make it more transparent and accessible. It is also a means for sharing knowledge about practice and considering jointly problems of practice. Like a medical round, in which different levels of expertise may be present, a Teacher Round incorporates multiple perspectives to bring more know-how to bear on the questions regarding practice which inevitably arise. And, also similar, a Teacher Round occurs in context, in real time. Both types of round link knowledge of a particular case to the development of practitioner knowledge more broadly. Both, finally, support the development of knowledge and practice as a collective action.

But the differences are significant. As Shulman (2004) pointed out, "The practice of teaching involves a far more complex task environment than does that of medicine" (p. 258). Knowing the individual is important to both teacher and physician, but teaching is complex precisely because a teacher is confronted with many learners and their various differences, whereas a physician normally can focus on one patient at a time. Cohen (2011) explains the complexity in terms of the "predicaments" of teaching, among them the "uncertainties and surprises" that arise due to its nature as a human endeavor. Teacher Rounds can unpack the complexity in a moment in time by bringing many eyes and ears to the process and can lead to greater insight on how to work within it. Moreover, Teacher Rounds can meet the need, in the face of teaching's complexity, for versatility, responsiveness, and adaptability in teaching practice by informing and building the practice repertoire of teachers—that is, by helping them to see and develop multiple ways of adjusting practice in view of the developmental, academic, cultural, and personal traits and needs of particular learners or groups of learners.

Potential Benefits of Teacher Rounds

A Teacher Round is designed to support collaborative teacher learning in, from, and about practice, in an actual classroom. It entails observation, reflection, and inquiry. While the primary actor is the teacher who hosts the Round in his or her classroom, a Teacher Round engages all participants in learning. Round participants stand to gain in developing acuity in close observation; in learning the value of descriptive rather than normative accounts of classroom activity; in grounding interpretation and assessment in observed evidence and contextual knowledge; in developing habits of reflection, personalization, and thoughtful inquiry over and against cursory judgment; in deepening understanding of the complexities and possibilities of practice as well as the work of particular learners; in the development of their own insight, practice, and expertise, including their repertoire of ways to understand and respond to different situations and different needs; and in their experience of a professional learning community.

Teacher Rounds bring teaching and learning into detailed focus. They help bind teachers together in a common effort to share and develop practice that works best for students. They help develop shared understandings of what learning that engages students fully looks like and what leads to it. In a given school, they can become a staple force in building and maintaining a student-centered professional learning community, as they are at University Park Campus School (see Chapter 5). Teacher Rounds can also play an integral role in teacher preparation, planned so as to support and guide students in their development as beginning teachers and collegial learners (see Appendix B).

This Book

This book is a conceptual and practical guide to Teacher Rounds. Its purpose is to explain and illustrate Teacher Rounds and their value in professional learning so that others may use them. It presents guidelines for practicing Teacher Rounds and illustrates them with examples involving both practicing and preservice teachers and what can be learned from them. Teacher Rounds can be implemented at any level and in virtually any setting. The detailed examples in the book are drawn from teachers, with varying degrees of experience, including teacher interns, working at the elementary, middle, and secondary levels in public urban schools that partner with me and my colleagues. As I mention in introducing the teachers and their school settings, the schools share a similar demographic profile, with large percentages of students who qualify for the federal free or reduced lunch program and who are nonnative English speakers.

Teacher Rounds are about teaching and learning; it is important, therefore, to articulate the relationship between the two. The first chapter offers a perspective on teaching and learning and how Teacher Rounds fit into it. After this conceptual beginning, Chapter 2 introduces the Teacher Round protocol—the step-by-step guide to a Teacher Round—and illustrates the steps in action. Chapters 3 and 4 offer detailed examples of Teacher Round learning at the high school and elementary levels, respectively. Although they are differentiated by school level, both chapters are relevant to understanding the Teacher Round process at any level. Chapter 5 portrays the Teacher Round learning process at University Park Campus School, an exemplary, high-performing urban secondary school which has long integrated Teacher Rounds into its professional learning culture. Drawing on the school's example, the chapter illustrates how Teacher Rounds can be used as a schoolwide practice by teachers and for teachers in order to build transparency, cohesion, coherence, and expertise in individual and collective practice. Chapter 6 explores more in-depth the processes of teacher inquiry, observation, and reflection that are so central to Teacher Round learning. The final chapter highlights what it takes to build a culture in which sharing and collaborating on the development of practice for the sake of student learning is a powerful norm. Appendices provide examples of start-up and preservice Teacher Round programs, as well as a convenient short version of the protocol. By the end, if you have come to value them, you should be fully ready to incorporate Teacher Rounds meaningfully into your own world of reflective practice.

Acknowledgments

I am fortunate to be able to work on a daily basis with dedicated principals, teachers, and teacher interns in schools serving students with a rich multiplicity of backgrounds in an urban neighborhood. They are committed equally to teaching, understanding their students' learning, and developing their practice. It is because of them and teachers like them that I am able to illustrate the power and potential of Teacher Rounds as a collaborative learning practice.

I would single out, first of all, my colleagues at University Park Campus School (UPCS), a school nationally recognized for its outstanding record in preparing its first-generation college students for postsecondary education, where Teacher Rounds are a normal part of school life. I appreciate greatly all of my colleagues there, in particular those teachers, both former and current, whose practice is represented in the book: Ricci Hall, Bob Knittle, Sarah Marcotte, Jim McDermott, Kevin Moylan, Kyle Pahigian, Meghan Rosa, Dan St. Louis, and Kate Shepard. I am grateful for many other teacher colleagues who so openly share their practice and experience of Teacher Rounds, especially those who appear in these pages: Jen Conlon and Sue Allen from Jacob Hiatt Elementary School, a school with a strong tradition of doing Teacher Rounds; Leann Ledoux and Tara Vaidya from South High School; and Margaret Welch from Woodland Academy.

My thanks go also to several principals who welcomed my participation in their first steps as they launched schoolwide Teacher Round programs: principal June Eressy, her assistant, Carenza Jackson, and their colleagues at Chandler Elementary School; principal Brad Morgan and colleagues at North Shore Technical High School; and Ricci Hall, principal, and his new colleagues at Claremont Academy, valued partners all. Thankfully, in addition, I was present when Kate Moylan talked about teaching until her "quads hurt."

Hundreds of teacher interns have been inducted into the Teacher Round process as they formed their own practice and learned to share, reflect on, and inquire into it with others. In their openness and commitment, they helped my colleagues and me to learn more about how to support them and to meet the challenges of teaching. I am grateful in particular for the several whose Teacher Round experience is represented in the book—Phoebe Cape, Jeremy Sanders, and Jeremy Murphy. My colleagues in the Adam Institute for Urban Teaching and School Practice, with whom I have participated in many a Teacher Round, have also helped me to understand the learning that can occur through the process. Thanks go in particular to Eric DeMeulenaere, Holly Dolan, Letina Jeranyama, Jim McDermott, Maureen Reddy, Heather Roberts, Raphael Rogers, Marlene Shepard, and Pete Weyler, as well as their predecessors, including Tom Berninghausen and Fiona McDonnell.

The seed for Teacher Rounds was planted many years ago in my own work, when the idea of doing something along the lines of medical rounds was suggested to me by then principal Arthur Bergeron and Superintendent John Collins of the Shrewsbury Public Schools. The idea took shape in collaboration with Arthur and his colleagues at the Coolidge Elementary School in the late 1980s. It gained maturity thanks to the colleagues whom I have already mentioned and others working alongside them. I am indebted to them all.

I express my gratitude for the service rendered by John Ameer and Jim McDermott in their honest appraisal of several draft chapters and for Dan Alpert, Senior Editor at Corwin Press, who believed in this book from the very beginning. Finally, I have had the great benefit of patient and loving support from my wife, Lena, particularly when I was thoroughly distracted by the work.

Publisher's Acknowledgments

Corwin gratefully acknowledges the contributions of the following reviewers:

Sherry Annee, Science Teacher
Brebeuf Jesuit Preparatory School
Indianapolis, IN

Amy Colton, Executive Director
Learning Forward Michigan
Ann Arbor, MI

Lois Easton, Educational Consultant and Author
LBE Learning
Tucson, AZ

Sue Elliott, Education Consultant
Suechelt Consulting
Sechelt, BC

Nina Morel, Associate Professor and Author
Lipscomb University, College of Education
Nashville, TN

Terry Morganti-Fisher, Educational Consultant
Learning Forward and QLD Learning
Austin, TX

Pamela R. Rosa, Core Service Director for Effective Professional Practice
Consortium for Educational Change
Lombard, IL

Christina M. Smith, Social Studies Dept. Chair
Algonquin Regional High School
Northborough, MA

Andrew Szczepaniak, Director, Professional Development
Gilbert Public Schools
Gilbert, AZ

Marion E. Woods, Director of Elementary Professional Development
Little Rock School District
Little Rock, AR

About the Author

Thomas Del Prete is the inaugural director of the Adam Institute for Urban Teaching and School Practice at Clark University in Worcester, MA. He is past director of the Hiatt Center for Urban Education at Clark and a former teacher of history and English at the middle and high school levels. He has worked for 25 years in teacher education, school-university partnership, and school reform. His previous books include *Improving the Odds: Developing Powerful Teaching Practice and a Culture of Learning in Urban High Schools* and *Thomas Merton and the Education of the Whole Person*. He has participated in hundreds of Teacher Rounds, most with his colleagues in the urban schools of Main South in Worcester, MA, in an effort to learn in and from practice.

1

The Practice of Teaching and Teacher Rounds

Aiming for the Sweet Spot

Teacher Rounds are meant to support teachers in understanding student learning and in developing their practice individually and collectively. Several fundamental questions, therefore, frame the work of Teacher Rounds: what do we teach for, and how do students learn deeply and well? How do our ideas about what we teach for and about learning shape teaching practice? How do we gain expertise in the practice of teaching, and what can school and other professional communities do to help develop effective practice? Big questions such as these do not always get the attention they deserve in the pressured world of teaching, professional learning, and accountability. This chapter starts from the premise that we need to consider them if we are to make professional learning—more specifically, Teacher Rounds—truly worthwhile and powerful. That said, the questions are challenging and complex: what follows is a broad response intended to put Teacher Rounds in larger perspective and encourage reflection and conversation.

What Do We Teach for and How Do Students Learn Deeply and Well?

Baseball players recognize the sound of the sweet spot, the deep resounding thwack that occurs when bat and ball meet true, propelling the ball outward with every bit of the force generated by the hitter. If there is a sweet spot in teaching, it may be at the point where the teacher gives a student or students just what they need to move forward on their own in purposeful and meaningful learning. Teachers and their students usually know when they are working well in the sweet spot: it is a space of optimal learning and growth, where students realize and exercise their full capability, and where teaching is equitable and learning rings authentic and true.

Thomas Merton (1958) wrote, "Your life is shaped by the end you live for." The same might be said about teaching: your teaching is shaped by the end you teach for. Teaching for the sweet spot is much different, certainly, from teaching for the test. In teaching for the sweet spot, teachers are not trying to run up a score but to support students in their full intellectual and personal development. To be sure, they want students to move forward in their learning and to develop important capabilities that standardized tests are meant to measure. But they do so by teaching for a quality of experience and breadth and depth of learning that respects and engages students fully as the young human beings they are.

What happens when students are learning in the sweet spot? First and foremost, they bring themselves fully and trustingly to learning, their whole attention absorbed in something interesting and meaningful. They work hard, maybe excitedly, to figure out something in the world of knowledge, to test ideas of their own, and to understand. They exercise their minds to the utmost, forming critical habits. They discover the efficacy of their own effort, perhaps in the face of a challenge that seemed daunting at the first moment of encounter, planting seeds of future commitment and persistence in learning. They experience, in an affirming way, their own capacities as learners and as people. In their work with others, they learn about the challenge and power of collaboration, communication, and community as well; they may even learn something about what they live for and how they can contribute to the well-being of the communities they live in. When teaching for the sweet spot, teachers support students in their personal and intellectual as well as knowledge development: they help them discover who they are and the persons they can be as well as what they can know and what they can do.

How Do Our Ideas About What We Teach for and About Learning Shape Teaching Practice?

Teaching for the sweet spot entails engaging and supporting all learners, with their different strengths, needs, personalities, social and cultural backgrounds, and dispositions, in meeting common learning goals, all in a particular social context and moment in time. Teachers call on different kinds of knowledge in this practice. They need to know what to give, how, and when. This knowing is an outgrowth of other knowing: knowing, first of all, their own beliefs and assumptions about learning; knowing students well and knowing, as it is often expressed, "where they are"—what they are thinking, feeling, and needing vis-à-vis their learning; knowing where, in terms of curriculum and learning goals, students need to go; and knowing pedagogy, content, and academic discipline with enough virtuosity and versatility to be able to create, at any given moment, in the face of student strength as well as need, a likely and meaningful path of learning for each student. Teachers, in other words, have to be equal parts passionate orchestrator and empathetic listener, thoughtful framer and strategic adaptor; they have to be nimble, shaping, yet at the same time, responding thoughtfully and purposefully, and occasionally with artful improvisation, to what is happening within the sphere of action defined by subject matter, students, and learning goals.

When teachers try to be otherwise, whether from conviction or to conform to an external mandate, when, for example, they try to approach learners and learning as if they can be subdued and herded down a single linear path, their effectiveness, ironically, is apt to get waylaid. Teaching for the sweet spot means supporting students on paths of learning that take into account who and where they are. It means opening and adjusting to the challenge, surprise, and the "uncertainty," as Cohen (2011) characterizes it, inherent in the process of engaging different minds and personalities in meaningful learning. In teaching, the unplanned and unexpected make regular appearances; the question for a teacher is what can be learned from them and how to respond. In this respect, teachers can claim some kinship with a batter in baseball: batters, too, must combine desire, skill, and judgment; calculating and adjusting as balls are thrown at different speeds, angles, and places with different motions by different pitchers at different times during the ebb and flow of the game; and decide in the moment whether a connection with the sweet spot of the bat is likely.

The multiple forms of knowledge that intertwine in teaching for the sweet spot can be called a teacher's knowledge and practice repertoire. A teacher's ability to adjust—to act so as to support particular students in the sweet spot of learning in a given moment—can be called adaptive expertise. More specifically, adaptive expertise refers to a teacher's ability to assess and respond effectively to what different students are thinking, doing, and needing, in a particular context (Darling-Hammond and Bransford, 2005, pp. 76–77). Figure 1.1 represents the interaction of these dimensions of teaching practice together with the critical processes that inform them—reflection and inquiry.

The dynamic of framing and adapting which characterizes a teacher's practice is very much in evidence in the Teacher Rounds presented throughout the book. Kate, for instance, must decide how to respond to a student's seemingly logical but faulty mathematical reasoning (see Chapter 2). Leann considers how to push for deeper analysis of literary theme in response to her students' comments (see Chapter 3). Margaret intervenes when a second grader struggles with a particular word during guided reading but refrains in another instance (Chapter 4). Momentarily at a loss, Sue must assess the value

Figure 1.1   Teaching for the Sweet Spot

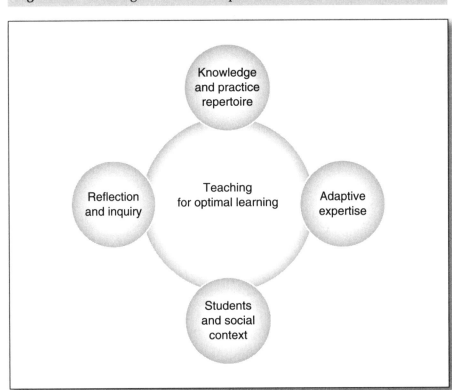

of pursuing her young students' utterly unexpected response to a reading (see Chapter 4). Kyle judges that a small group's struggle is productive and decides to affirm their effort and draw back rather than provide explicit guidance (see Chapter 5). The Teacher Round process helps draw attention to challenging and consequential moments of decision making such as these; it focuses many eyes and ears on the thinking and action involved, helping to make the learning of students and the practice of teaching more transparent. In other words, it engages the knowledge and practice repertoires and adaptive expertise of participants. There is much at work in the process: Teacher Rounds help teachers practice and develop the habits, skills, and knowledge which teachers call on as they frame and adapt to student learning; the habits, skills, and knowledge which help them better understand and respond constructively to what students are thinking, doing, and needing.

Habits, Skills, and Knowledge of Effective Practice

In responding and adapting to what they see, hear, and learn in their classrooms, teachers such as Kate, Leann, Margaret, Sue, and Kyle consider the present need in light of their prior experience and knowledge—they engage in a process of reflection. In their effort to understand where students are they use personalization skills: they observe, they attend closely, they inquire into, and they assess individual student learning. In facilitating different ways for students to support each other's learning and to learn together, they foster and tap the power of the class as a learning community. Understanding these ingredients of teaching expertise will help in understanding the Teacher Round process and its potential to inform and develop practice.

Reflection

In the actual act of teaching, the process that teachers use in responding to what students are thinking and doing can be described, in the terms used by Schon (1983) in *The Reflective Practitioner,* as "reflection-in-action." They are responding to "the unique case" defined by each student's or student group's particular interaction with subject matter (p.68). John Dewey (1938) might add that this reflective process entails both "observation and memory," as teachers try to understand and respond to the present case in light of prior experience (p. 64). They construct, in Schon's words, a theory of the unique case, act on it in a way calculated to support student engagement and learning, and in learning from what happens, swing or miss, go about adding knowledge to memory; in other words, go about building adaptive expertise.

All the basic forms of knowledge that teachers use—knowledge about students, subject matter, pedagogy, context, and their own assumptions—enter into the reflective process and determine the potential effectiveness of a teacher's adaptive action. In a Teacher Round, teachers have an opportunity individually and together to understand and learn from this internal dynamic of practice. They do this partly by practicing some of the personalization skills which build personal knowledge about students and the ability to support them.

Personalization

Education, in its Latin origin, means to draw out, not to pour in. In this sense, education is profoundly personal: there is something in all of us worth every effort of drawing out. Call it, perhaps, our individual genius, that combination of unique and shared capacities that we all have which are worth discovering, cultivating, refining, expressing, and contributing as part of our development as educated persons in a democratic society. It is one of the joys of teaching to see evidence of these capacities emerging every day—a sudden or slowly nurtured insight, a conviction formed from careful study, a shy but perceptive voice, or an idea of what makes something work or what might make something work better. Teachers draw them out all the time: teaching is preeminently a personal and personalizing process.

Personalization starts with regard for each student as a whole thinking and feeling person full of personal capabilities and cultural strengths, full of hopes, feelings, predilections, and wonderful, perhaps yet-to-be-discovered, potentials; and with concern for the well-being and learning of each student. In personalizing, teachers strive to know each student well and to understand what each is thinking and doing in the context of classroom learning and, to some extent, why. This knowledge informs a teacher's effort to engage students trustingly, fully, and meaningfully in learning; it also informs the effort to harness the strengths of each student in support of the learning of his or her peers and the classroom community as a whole.

The great educator, Horace Mann, sheds light on what personalization in teaching means. In 1840, in a passage remarkable for its pedagogical insight, especially for its time, he wrote,

... the mind of a teacher should migrate, as it were, into those of his pupils, to discover what they know and feel and need; and then, supplying from his own stock, what they require, he should reduce it to such a form, and bring it within such a distance, that they can reach out and seize and appropriate it. (as cited in Cremin, 1957, p. 46)

Tolstoy, who started a school for peasant children in mid-nineteenth century Russia, had a similar idea: "The best teacher will be he who has at his tongue's end the explanation of what is bothering the pupil. These explanations give the teacher the greatest possible number of methods, the ability of inventing new methods and, above all, not a blind adherence to one method . . ." (as cited in Schon, 1983, p. 66).

Both Tolstoy and Mann imagined a personalized pedagogy, one consistent with the sweet spot of learning. Both anticipate later theories of learning, such as Dewey's progressivism and Piaget's constructivism, in which students are seen as active knowers and the teacher is a keenly observant and active supporter, in which practice is molded by what and how students are learning. They both also set a high standard: to determine the "mind" of a student in the sense of discovering what each knows and feels and needs, and to respond constructively, requires considerable attentiveness, empathy, and adaptive expertise. The teacher, therefore, must follow in order to lead; is cast as a guide who, paradoxically, follows the path of students' learning—their minds and dispositions as they navigate the terrain of subject matter—in order to determine how to help them go further. "Mind reading," in a certain sense, is one of the challenges that a teacher concerned about the learning of each student must strive to meet.

Teacher Rounds, structured so as to bring multiple eyes and ears to bear in understanding students' learning and what supports it, ask each participant to practice, to some degree, the critical skills involved in personalization as Mann and Tolstoy understood it: close observation, together with its indispensable allies—attending, empathizing and relating, assessing, and inquiring.

Observing, attending, empathizing and relating. Dig into the root meanings of observation and attentiveness and one finds that they are closely linked terms: observation derives partly from the idea of "attending to." To attend to something means combining observation with care and thoughtfulness; it means an effort to relate, to take an empathetic stance to students' learning, to try to grasp their experience intuitively as well as intellectually and to step momentarily into their shoes. Openness and empathy help in transcending any intellectual or personal bias that might prejudice a teacher's effort to understand what different students are thinking, doing, and needing.

The poetry of Mary Oliver, so full of natural images etched in wonder, as if they were newly born, suggests what openness and attentiveness in a classroom can mean. She declares that paying attention "is our endless and proper work." "How important it is," she writes, "to walk along, not in haste but slowly, looking at everything . . ." (Oliver, 2003). For Oliver, to be attentive in the world means to look at everything so as to let it in as it really is, so as to see it in its wonderful fullness. In a similar way, paying attention in the classroom means momentarily suspending or at least constraining our predispositions about what students might or should be thinking; it means increasing the possibility for seeing and hearing what the student really knows, feels, and needs or, at the very least, for identifying what in a student's thinking would be helpful to understand better, paving the way for inquiry. "Pay attention. Be astonished. Talk about it," Oliver exhorts in another poem (Oliver, 2008).

So often, observation in classrooms means something much more limited—cataloguing, for example, what students or teachers do or say. While this approach often yields helpful information, it stays more or less on the surface of what is possible to know. For example, we may be able to count the number of students who are searching in a text for some information to confirm or disconfirm an idea, but are we able to say how they are making sense of what they are reading—how they are constructing the meaning of the text? We may be able to determine how many students provide an answer, but can we say how each one came to it and what each understands, and what meaning each student's method of understanding might hold for others and the work of teaching-learning? We might be able to talk about who was right and wrong, but can we identify learning opportunities gained or lost, and how?

When observing, attending, and relating, a teacher might not be astonished, in the sense that Mary Oliver uses the word, by a student's intuition or glimmering of understanding or insightful question, but might be enlightened. There are numerous examples of such teacher enlightenment, and most teachers can point to their own. Consider, for example, Vivian Paley's warm and astute observations of young children at play, which led her to understand the powerful learning that occurs through storytelling: "Above all, I think, the continued observation of children at play demonstrates the importance of make-believe as the thinking tool children use" (as cited in National

Association for the Education of Young Children, 2001). Or consider the insights of Lisa Delpit, who reminds us in her most recent book to heed and leverage all that children, who may not come to school with the skills typical of middle class children, "*do* know and bring with them to class," such as "maturity in problem-solving, an ability to do what is needed in difficult situations, an understanding of real-world problems" (Delpit, 2012). Teachers who appear in the chapters that follow, such as Kate, Leann, Sue, Margaret, and Kyle, are keen to know and support the capabilities, approaches to learning, and developing minds of their students, and invite their colleagues to help through Teacher Rounds.

Assessing and personalizing: Exercising our "quads." Assessment, evaluation, and testing often get conflated, as if they all mean the same thing. But assessment in its original and intended sense, as reflected in its root meaning of "sitting by," has little to do with the other two. Assessment is one of the skills teachers use to personalize. In assessing students, teachers sit literally and figuratively beside them so as to have the best possible vantage point for understanding what and how they are thinking and what they need. Expressing this view, Kate, a high school history teacher, says she has her best days teaching when her "quads hurt" (K. Moylan, personal communication, May 23, 2012). Teaching so that one's quads hurt is not simply an intellectual matter. In sitting by their students, teachers communicate their regard, respect, and commitment and learn to relate; they build trust. They learn firsthand some or all of what they need to address in order to sustain students in the optimal zone of their own learning, so that they develop understanding, capability, and a sense of self-efficacy.

When teachers attend caringly and openly to the learning of students—to what and how they are thinking in relation to the subject matter at hand, to what they respond to and engage in, to what supports and challenges them, to what they struggle with and why— they value and make students' explanations of their ideas and how they arrived at them a normal occurrence. They follow students' personal paths of learning and map out likely ways for them to move forward toward greater subject matter understanding and appreciate and relate more fully to who they are. The student's experience, too, is transformed: if their engaged thoughts and experience have such importance, then so in a profound sense, do they; and so might their learning be that much more worth pursuing, be worth a few swings and misses of their own.

In the process of Teacher Rounds, where the work of observing, attending, empathizing, relating, assessing, and mapping out is momentarily shared, teachers may not only develop knowledge of student learning meaningful in the context of a specific class but also generate insight into curricular and learning possibilities with wider application—for starters, in the practice of other Teacher Round participants and their classrooms. The Rounds Day at University Park Campus School, portrayed in Chapter 5, illustrates this potential.

Inquiry. Focused inquiry is a powerful tool in a teacher's effort to understand an individual learner or group of learners and teaching-learning more generally. Focused inquiry means turning learning and practice goals, observations, intuitions, and reflections—including challenges, theories about what will engage particular students, certainties and uncertainties, puzzlements about student engagement or performance, disappointments, concerns, hopes, and, yes, astonishment and wonderment—into questions and finding ways to answer them in a particular moment or over time. When teachers inquire, they become deeper learners of student learning, as well as of curriculum and teaching; they tap the potential to learn in and from practice.

Inquiry into student learning and teaching practice, in its actual context, is an essential component of Teacher Rounds. The Round Teacher, the teacher who hosts the Round in her or his classroom, formulates the Round inquiry, literally a set of questions or directions on what to look, listen, or ask for in the course of teaching-learning, as described in the next chapter. A teacher's Round inquiry usually links to learning goals, observations, and assessments about particular student's learning, or to particular practices or aspects of practice. The inquiry helps members of the Round group act as collaborative observers working to uncover and understand what is happening and to what effect.

Turning Classrooms into Authentic Learning Communities

It is not possible, of course, to attend closely to every student in a class of students at every moment. But, teachers can create moments for attending closely and can implement ways to elicit student thinking, to make it visible. Furthermore, they can enlist students as witting or unwitting accomplices, in the process helping them to clarify and sharpen their own thoughts and ideas, and become respectful cobuilders of a community of mutual inquirers and knowledge seekers.

Students become willing collaborators in their teacher's effort to understand and respond constructively to what they know, feel, and need, to the extent they learn to trust that who they are, including their ideas as well as their confusions, will be respected, and that they are considered a valued part of the learning process; to the extent they learn increasingly to explain their reasoning and listen to each other's ideas and ask for clarification as needed; to the extent they develop the habit of recognizing and using appropriate evidence to support their reasoning and to fulfill a commitment to know honestly and truthfully; to the extent they develop the habit of digging out and questioning their own assumptions; to the extent that they have multiple opportunities and ways to express what they understand and know and are unsure about; in other words, to the extent that they are part of an authentic thinking community.

Teachers turn classrooms into thinking communities in which every student's thinking is valued and made visible to the teacher and peers in manifold ways. Walk into Jill's 4th grade classroom, and pairs of students are reading passages to each other from books they have chosen to read, each time explaining what they understand or do not understand, what connections they make to their own experience or previous reading, and what questions they have. In Kate's 8th grade mathematics classroom, you might ask a student to share a "Dear Confused" letter he or she is writing to explain how to solve a math problem to "Confused"—a fictional creation who is stymied for one reason or another. Listen intently in Pete's 9th grade English class, and you might be discomfited by long moments of silence that are a normal part of learning there, as student thinking gestates or gets formed in the process of trying to write it down. Sit beside a small group of students who are in Meghan's 12th grade English class reading Shakespeare's *Hamlet*. You will hear each share a question for peer consideration that grows out of some specific confusion or musing each had in comprehending the language, the storyline, the character's development, or some thematic element (see discussion of one of Meghan's Teacher Rounds in Chapters 5 and 6). Each of these moments affords an opportunity for the teacher to listen to and to see manifestations of student thinking; in other words, to migrate into their minds, just as they are, with the same attentiveness that the poet Mary Oliver has for the world that she has learned to let in and relate to, just as it is.

How Do Teachers Develop Expertise?

Learning how to hit a baseball on the sweet spot of the bat with some consistency requires enormous dedication as well as patience. Hitters learn partly by approximation, swinging and missing one time, and recalibrating for the next. Their practice entails considerable study and reflection as well as repeated action and experience, as they learn the art of the pitcher and refine as necessary their approach. Since hitting is a very public act, there is ample opportunity for hitters to share and discuss their experience with observant colleagues and, through analysis and reflection, to build the knowledge which will inform their next instant of judgment at the plate.

Teachers, too, whether preservice or in-service, need opportunities to practice, analyze, inquire into, and reflect on their teaching with others. This, in fact, is a core principle of what Richard Elmore (2004) refers to as a "consensus view" of powerful teacher learning. The consensus view holds that "teachers learn through social interaction around problems of practice" and that the development of new practices requires "support for collegial interaction . . ." (p. 109). This widely accepted principle is exemplified in the standards of Learning Forward (2012), a leading organization in the field that emphasizes the importance of "learning communities committed to continuous improvement, collective responsibility, and goal alignment." In the paradigm of professional learning espoused by Learning Forward, teachers are active and central figures; they help determine what learning will be most beneficial and how.

The Challenge of Collaborative Learning

As much as teacher collaboration focused on enhancing practice and student learning is valued, it is has yet to be fully established as the norm of professional learning; nor necessarily is it effective when it is implemented (see discussion in Fullan, 2007). There are a host of factors that help explain the challenge of effective implementation and that are helpful to know in thinking about how to integrate collaborative learning practices such as Teacher Rounds fruitfully into professional life: collaboration must confront a stubborn pattern of teacher isolation in the profession; collaboration must have the concerted and sustained support that organizations such as Learning Forward recognize as essential components of success; collaboration must connect to what matters in practice and pass the bottom-line test of enhancing the learning of students.

Among the historical and cultural factors, the theme of teacher isolation stands out. For reasons that have as much to do with the way a teacher's day is structured and the way the work of teaching has been conceived as with the psychological vulnerability of teachers, the profession has had difficulty evolving a culture and practice of working together. In his classic study, *Schoolteacher,* Lortie (1975) delineated some of the colluding and constraining forces, which reverberate still. These include a teacher's overriding concern, in the face of uncertainty and challenge, for what will serve immediate needs ("presentism"); loyalty, partly out of concern for securing the present, to the status quo ("conservatism"); and a tendency, fed by the other two forces, to keep the classroom door closed ("individualism").

Lortie's study spawned considerable effort, in the name of school reform, to break through teacher isolation and establish more collegial norms of behavior; the prevailing theory of change, according to Hargreaves (2010), was "Eliminate individualism and you cure conservatism." But, as Hargreaves and others have learned, this formula can be applied simplistically, with zeal to promote collaboration resulting in forced or highly directed teaming, or what Hargreaves labels "contrived collegiality." When teacher collaboration is subject to top-down control, increased standardization of curriculum and teaching, and narrow accountability measures, then teachers have more reason to resist than to participate. Imposed collaboration can foster more conservative individual behavior even as it feeds a less collegial, less democratic, more conservative institutional philosophy. Students' education can suffer as much as teacher professionalism under these circumstances.

There is a cautionary tale in the work of Hargreaves and others for those who would support teacher collaboration. Collaboration by itself will not enhance teacher learning any more than it will student learning. Collaboration needs a valued common purpose, some measure of self-direction, and shared responsibility and accountability. It needs to start with and nourish trust among participants and trust between teachers and any overarching leadership or institutional structure (Bryk and Schneider, 2002). It needs to be founded on respect for teachers as professionals and for the challenging work of teaching. It should enable teachers to act with vocational integrity and build a common approach to equitable practice. Principles such as these are part of the consensus view of professional learning designed to improve student learning.

Examples of powerful collaborative learning experiences for teachers are documented in the literature. A report from The National

Commission on Teaching and America's Future (Carroll, Thomas, Fulton, and Doerr, 2010) testifies to the strong positive relationship between valued teacher collaboration and student performance. In a similar vein, Hargreaves (2010) reports on work in Finland, where teachers participate in a largely self-regulated collaborative culture. Recent work by Troen and Boles (2012) on the power of teacher teaming adds to this growing body of testimonials. The challenge is to make these documented positive experiences the norm of professional life in schools—to turn Lortie's triad of presentism, individualism, and conservatism into reflective action, genuine collaboration, and progressivism. The critical work, in other words, is to help teachers develop learning communities which enable them to learn in, from, and about their own practice in relation to student learning; it is equally important for those preparing to become teachers to learn in such communities (See Appendix B). The Teacher Round process can play a significant role in this work.

Teacher Rounds and Collaborative Learning in and From Practice

The Teacher Round process provides a focused and grounded way for teachers to share, develop, and understand practice in relation to how and what their students are learning. It is distinguished as a collaborative learning practice in that it takes teachers directly into their classrooms, into the heart of the dynamic of teaching and learning—of framing and adapting, of personalizing and reflective action. The process engages and contributes directly to the development of knowledge and practice repertoires and adaptive expertise. It supports the development of a community of reflective and shared practice among teachers and helps teachers understand and develop a powerful parallel learning culture for their students.

Teacher Rounds play this role at University Park Campus School (see Chapter 5), where they occur routinely. Teachers at the school trust and value Teacher Rounds as a powerful mode of colearning and mutual support. This view prevails partly because important conditions for collaborative teacher learning are met there. Most notably, teachers as well as students are valued as thinkers and central actors in their respective realms of work, and teacher learning at the school is centered on students and their learning. As a result, Teacher Rounds do not stand alone in supporting professional learning. They are aligned with other collaborative efforts: teachers regularly examine student work and evaluate student progress together and use what they learn to plan and implement strategies for supporting students within and across grade levels. They also coplan curriculum and have developed their own criteria for evaluating their classroom practice.

Teacher Rounds, like any form of teacher collaboration, fulfill their potential to enhance the knowledge, habits, skills, and development of practice when, as at University Park Campus School, there is mutual agreement among all concerned on their purpose, their value, and how they will be carried out; when, in effect, there is a professional compact. Figure 1.2 provides a sample of what teachers, school leaders, preservice students and their mentors, and other collaborators might discuss and agree to.

Harvesting the Wisdom of Practice

We live during a time in which technology, so impressive in its capacities, increasingly interconnects with our lives. No doubt influenced by the allure of what technology can do, we have become increasingly accustomed to thinking in terms of technical solutions

Figure 1.2   Sample Teacher Rounds Compact

As collaborators in professional learning, we pledge to:

- respect and maintain our integrity as teachers, that is, the integrity of the teaching vocation;
- conduct Teacher Rounds solely for the purpose of learning in and from practice together about all students and their learning and what supports it;
- strive in our learning together to:
  - o understand our beliefs, goals, and rationales and how they are manifest in our teaching;
  - o mutually develop essential habits and skills of practice, including reflection, observation, attentiveness, relating, assessing, and inquiry;
  - o develop our understanding of what defines, creates, and sustains a zone of optimal and powerful learning for each and every student;
  - o share and develop our knowledge and practice repertoires and adaptive expertise—that is, our ways to frame, understand, and respond to what students are learning and need in order to help them to move forward for good purpose on their own; and
  - o help each other work in the sweet spot of teaching and learning;
- strive to build trust, openness, and a community of reflective practice through our colearning; and
- model for students the attitudes, beliefs, expectations, and habits of a strong culture of learning.

to problems. Sometimes we conflate technical and technological with scientific, to make them thereby somehow more credible; science may inform technological improvement and vice versa but by no stretch do they mean the same thing. Sometimes a solution that is not technical is deemed to be deficient, unworthy of serious consideration. This line of thinking can lead to oversimplification of complex problems and complex practices such as teaching. Indeed, the work of teaching has not been immune to the bias towards technical solutions in the culture. Together with the influence gained by a corporate command-and-control model of institutional behavior, the idea that teaching-learning can be subject to a technical and testable process of evaluation and improvement has carried considerable weight in educational policymaking.

But, as characterized in this chapter, teaching is a complex and contextual practice and preeminently a reflective, dynamic, personal, and communal one. To treat it simply as a technical practice reduces its wonderful and rich human complexity and challenge, reduces its potential to touch each student's life significantly and profoundly, and reduces the idea of education to mere training. Teaching is learning everyday—with a fair share of swings and misses—how to engage and contribute to the development of the minds of particular students and their capacities as human beings. Such immediate work is framed by curricular expectations and understandings, such as the Common Core State Standards, and can be informed tremendously by more distant work—by the insights and knowledge of others. But, within its guiding frameworks, the practice of teaching is developed through felt and carefully reflected-upon experience, a process that becomes more informing to the extent that it is carried out with others attuned to its complexity, possibility, and everyday context, and who work collaboratively, in intentional ways, to learn in and from it.

What teachers learn individually and together by exercising habits of reflection, personalization, and inquiry builds their knowledge and practice repertoires and adaptive expertise, taps and develops, borrowing from Lee Shulman (2004), the wisdom of practice. As teachers' understanding of the possible pathways of student learning grows, they can better relate to what and how each student is engaged; as their repertoire of ways for responding to and guiding students on their pathways grows, they are better able to keep students in a zone of optimal and purposeful learning; as their capability to work with students both individually and in groups grows, they are better able to help build their capacities as learners who increasingly can help themselves and each other.

Not all practice is wise. But, as on the baseball field, there is wisdom in practice that aims for the sweet spot and wisdom, too, in working together carefully to harvest it. The Teacher Round protocol, explained in the next chapter, is meant to be a collaborative harvesting tool.

Questions to Consider

- With what do we agree or disagree with respect to the view of teaching and learning presented in this chapter? What would we change or add?
- What is our view of powerful student learning? What does it look and sound like?
- What does teaching centered on the sweet spot of practice look like?
- What powerful teaching and learning practices will we try to implement and learn more about through the Teacher Round process?
- What will be our "Teacher Round compact?"

2

The Teacher Round Protocol

Many teachers have a running conversation with colleagues about their teaching and learning experiences. Their conversations are filled with anecdotes expressing wonder, confusion, joy, puzzlement, determination, questions, theories, and musing, all in some way connected to their effort to understand their students and what might best engage and support them in learning. Protocols, such as those which help teachers look at student work or structure an inquiry based on some problem of practice, take these corridor and lunchtime conversations and turn them into a more formal learning process. They encourage disciplined, in-depth, productive collegial discussion and problem solving. They "force transparency" (McDonald, Mohr, Dichter, and McDonald, 2003). That is, they help bring to the surface various aspects of practice and the reasoning behind them, as well as some of the intricacies of student learning, opening them for examination and reflection.

The Teacher Round protocol serves this general purpose of protocols for professional learning. It is distinctive in that it is constructed specifically to foster collaborative learning both in and from practice, in context, in real time. It also encompasses a full episode of teaching-learning, brings into focus the knowledge repertoire and adaptive expertise of practice, and incorporates habits of personalization, inquiry, and reflection. By following the Teacher Round protocol, participants tap the potential of Teacher Rounds to build understanding relevant to a particular teacher and classroom, as well as to maintain and develop more generally their own practice. The Teacher Round protocol is also adaptable to more specific purposes, such as enacting a particular curricular philosophy or addressing a commonly defined problem, held by a group of teachers, an entire school faculty, a preservice teacher preparation group, or some networked combination of teachers and other educators.

Preparing for Teacher Rounds

Preparation for implementing the Teacher Round protocol may include teachers working together to:

- ✓ Establish shared ideas about teaching and learning, using questions such as those listed at the conclusion of Chapter 1
- ✓ Develop or review (if one has been adopted) their Teacher Round compact (see Chapter 1)
- ✓ Clarify any specific purposes for the Teacher Rounds (see below)
- ✓ Ensure shared understanding of the general characteristics of Teacher Rounds (see page 20)
- ✓ Determine who will participate in the Teacher Round (see page 21)
- ✓ Determine a schedule for the first Teacher Round (see page 22)

What Are the Specific Purposes of Teacher Rounds?

A Teacher Round easily stands alone as a meaningful experience of learning in and from practice: a teacher shares his or her practice, and colleagues participate in the effort to learn collaboratively. Each subsequent Teacher Round builds the culture of sharing, reflection, inquiry, and collaboration, and supports the development of adaptive expertise. Teacher Rounds also complement or integrate readily into other colearning. Teachers in study or critical friend groups, collaborating on lesson study, or working together on grade-level and vertical teams, for example, can incorporate Teacher Rounds into their learning process.

When conducted in a school, partnership, or network in a coordinated manner, rather than as single events, Teacher Rounds may have any of a number of specific purposes in mind:

- To better understand ways to include, engage, and support a particular group of students served by a team of teachers
- To share and inquire into an instructional practice or particular approach to learning, for example, guided reading or collaborative investigations in science
- To address school improvement goals, such as increasing the reading and writing proficiency of English learners
- To share and develop practice consistent with a school's learning philosophy and common core curriculum goals
- To share and inquire into ways to support students' development as active and inquiring learners in a discipline (for example, helping students learn to critically examine primary sources in history or helping them to turn one of their questions into a testable hypothesis and experiment in science)
- To address a particular question or challenge of practice shared by a group of teachers or by an entire school—for example, how to integrate English learners fully into classroom learning— bringing multiple perspectives to bear on it
- To share and build a common understanding of how to support students' development as academic learners ready for college within or across grade levels
- To develop the habit of reflective practice

Starting fresh with Teacher Rounds, a group of teachers might simply want to get used to the process and develop the habit of sharing and reflecting on their practice together before setting more specific agendas (See Appendix A for specific examples of how schools have introduced the Teacher Rounds process). In any case, teachers should be clear on what they aim to achieve during the initial stage of implementing a Teacher Rounds program.

What Are the Key Characteristics of a Teacher Round?

- A Teacher Round occurs in a real everyday context, in an actual classroom, in real time.
- A Teacher Round is about learning in and from practice. It is not a process of evaluation.
- A Teacher Round is always framed by the Round teacher— the teacher who prepares and hosts the Round in her or his

classroom. The Round teacher, however, may have a collaborator or two, or a thought partner.

- A Teacher Round is a collaborative process—a way to bring extra eyes and ears to the task of learning what students are thinking and doing and what is engaging them and to what end.
- A Teacher Round involves a minimum of three and up to seven or so teachers (including the Round Teacher) or some combination of teachers and other educators (for example, preservice teachers, a school adjustment counselor, a principal, or a faculty member from a college partner). Having at least 3 to 4 participants ensures that a range of experience and multiple perspectives are brought to the process.
- A Teacher Round always entails intentional reflection, observation, inquiry, and collaboration. Round participants are reflective partners.

Who Will Participate and When?

In deciding who will attend a school's or a group's first Teacher Round, one point is critical: it is vitally important that Teacher Rounds and any formal teacher evaluation remain separate. One question also is pivotal: who is ready to uphold the Teacher Round compact or otherwise act so as to safeguard and fulfill the purposes of the Teacher Round? Planners might also ask where trust is already high or likely to grow. Depending on the school or context, the answer to these questions might mean that teachers, coaches, and administrators will all participate, that a pilot group, with a mix of personnel, will begin, or that a self-selected group of teachers only will participate, with administrators providing logistical support. In subsequent chapters, you will learn about different examples, such as the whole school approaches at Jacob Hiatt Elementary School (Chapter 4), University Park Campus School (Chapter 5), and Claremont Academy and Chandler Elementary School (Appendix A).

There is, of course, another layer of participation—the students themselves. Teachers hosting a Teacher Round prepare their students in different ways. Some will say that the visiting teachers are interested in learning about what students are doing and may ask students to explain their learning to them. Some will mention further the Teacher Round concept and how it represents teachers collaborating to learn just as they ask students to do, in this way reinforcing the culture and practice of learning in their schools. When Teacher Rounds have become a customary practice, then only newly arriving students in a school need any introduction.

The Teacher Round Protocol

A Teacher Round has four integral parts and an optional fifth part:

1. Preparation of the Round sheet

2. The preround orientation

3. The Round (when the Teacher Round group actually observes teaching-learning)

4. The postround reflection

5. The Teacher Round follow-up (optional)

The preround orientation and postround reflection, in particular, may be facilitated, moderated, or self-moderated. If facilitated, the facilitator guides the Round teacher and Round partners through each step. If moderated, the moderator is a member of the Round group designated to pay attention to the group's progress in following the protocol, to remind the group of each step, and to help pace the group in the time allotted. If self-moderated, Round partners share or divide up responsibility for the functions of the moderator. In every case, Round partners take coresponsibility for upholding their Teacher Round compact, if one has been adopted, and for fulfilling the general and specific purposes of the Teacher Round.

Part 1 of the Teacher Round Protocol: Preparing the Round Sheet

The Round sheet plays a vital role for the Round teacher and his or her Round partners. First of all, it is an invitation to learn in and from the practice of the Round teacher. It starts the process of opening up—making transparent—and examining practice by explaining the planning of the Round teacher. It opens up practice as well by inquiring into it—by asking specific questions to draw attention to what students are doing or saying in relation to curriculum material, to structures meant to support student participation, to particular tasks and students' engagement with them, and to teacher actions. It sets the stage for collaborative learning in the Round.

The Round sheet is an act of reflection and inquiry, not a lesson plan. Preparing it encourages the Round teacher to review her or his planning reflectively: what he or she has planned for this day and why (what assumptions and theory of learning underlie and inform the plan); how learning goals, subject matter, and planned activities each makes sense in light of the others; and how and why different students will be meaningfully engaged, supported, and challenged. Preparation also encourages the Round teacher to think about what others need to know in order to enter the classroom having a clear idea of what the teacher and students will be doing. Finally, the Round sheet asks the teacher to form an inquiry focused on aspects of the teaching and learning worth attending to closely in order to understand what happens and its significance.

Part of the function of the Round sheet, then, is to establish the host teacher's frame of reference for members of the Round group; it puts teaching and learning in context. It is important for Round partners to understand the Round teacher's understanding of curriculum, students, and practice. It may also be very helpful to understand the Round teacher's understanding of goals, tools, or questions of practice shared by members of the Round group. By entering, to the extent possible, the Round teacher's frame of reference, Round partners not only show respect for a colleague, they loosen whatever hold their own preconceptions and predisposed way of seeing may have on them as observers. They also acquire enough specific contextual knowledge to talk about practice in the postround discussion in a way that connects constructively to the perspective of the host teacher. Their understanding of frame of reference and context helps them to become reflective partners in learning.

In sum, the Round sheet offers a simple guide for learning in and from a specific instance of practice. It points the way for reflection, observation, inquiry, and collaboration to come together. Even with this broad purpose in mind, a typical Round sheet will take up no more than two sides of paper, including ample space for notes beneath each of the typically 3 to 5 Round questions. The Round sheet should be succinct; there is opportunity during the preround orientation, described below, to clarify and elaborate what is on it, as needed.

Round sheet sections

The Round sheet includes three sections: background, learning focus, and Round inquiry.

Background (what, who, and why). The background section sets the curricular, academic, and social context of the Round—the what, who, and why. This is an opportunity for the Round teacher to inform members of the Round group about the curricular material and how it is unfolding; about relevant prior work and the development of student understanding; about characteristics of individual learners or the class as a whole that she or he has taken into account in planning; and what theory of learning, research, and wisdom of practice informs the plan. Essential questions for the Round Teacher are, *"What do my Round partners need to know in order to understand what I have planned and why it makes sense—why it creates a zone of optimal learning—for these students at this moment? What do they need to know in order to understand what students will be thinking about and doing?"*

The following more specific questions may also help guide teachers in writing the background section:

- The curriculum and how it is unfolding
  - Where does this lesson fit in the overall roll-out of the curriculum?
  - What particular curricular principles and standards am I addressing in the lesson?
- Relevant prior work and student understanding
  - What understanding of the subject matter are students bringing to the lesson, based on their prior work?
  - What, if anything, has challenged or puzzled some or all students up to this point?
  - What information about relevant student work am I taking into account in planning the scaffolding and structure for learning?
- Characteristics of individual learners or the class as a learning community
  - What attributes or particular questions about individual learners am I considering in planning the lesson?
  - What norms or habits of learning in the class as a whole, if any, am I counting on or trying to cultivate?
- Theory of learning, research, or wisdom of practice
  - Why do I believe that what I have planned will provide a meaningful and valuable learning experience for all students and achieve my learning goals?
  - What key idea(s) about learning and practice is informing or reflected in my lesson?
  - What am I concerned or unsure about?

Round learning focus. A Teacher Round ultimately turns on the question of student learning and how it relates to teaching practice. In the Round learning focus section the Round teacher explains the student learning planned for the day. The Round teacher also identifies the focus of professional learning for the Round.

If the Teacher Round is part of a series with a specific purpose or theme—an interest or concern about student learning, curriculum, or practice—that is shared by Round colleagues, then the learning focus would be crafted accordingly. During a "Rounds day" at University Park Campus School (UPCS), for example, teachers shared an interest in understanding how, and with what effect, the framework for instruction they hold in common is being enacted in different classrooms across grade levels (see Chapter 5). In their first series of Teacher Rounds at Chandler Elementary School, intermediate grade teachers focused on their efforts to enhance their students' development as readers and writers (see Appendix A).

Here are several questions for teachers to consider in developing the Round learning focus:

- Learning-centered
  - On what learning goals am I centrally focused in this lesson? What specifically is the process of learning that students will be engaged in? What can my Round partners expect to see or hear to indicate that students are learning in line with the learning goals? How would I know whether each student is working in what for him or her is a zone of optimal learning?
- Practice-centered
  - What in particular about the teaching-learning am I trying to learn about or understand better with my Teacher Round partners? Is there some aspect of practice whose effectiveness I want to understand—what would help me to understand it?

Round inquiry. The Round teacher frames the inquiry for the Teacher Round. Generally, this means turning the Round learning focus into a set of questions or directions on what to look and listen for, or ask students about, in order to understand the teaching-learning. The inquiry is vital in terms of focusing Teacher Round learning and directing the attention of Teacher Round participants during the Round. The key challenge is to frame the inquiry so that Teacher Round partners are able to gather concrete evidence, through attentive observation, on what students or the teacher do or say relative to the learning focus.

The Round Teacher does not need to carry the burden of forming the Round inquiry entirely alone. Colleagues are Round accomplices.

Colleagues can be consulted in constructing the Round sheet. And during the preround orientation they can help to clarify the inquiry and sharpen the Round group's readiness to observe and attend in a way that will shed light on learning and on practice.

Even with collaborative effort, however, the formation of a Round inquiry which is meaningful and focuses attention on appropriate evidence may need considerable practice (see Chapter 6). And more practiced Round teachers may over time strive for questions aimed at uncovering more subtle aspects of learning. Here are some basic questions to consider in framing the Round inquiry:

- o What are one or more things that I really want to understand about my lesson, keeping in mind the goal of ensuring optimal learning for all of my students?
- • Students' intellectual engagement
  - o What would I look, listen, or ask for in order to know that students are engaged in thinking and acting in line with my learning focus?
  - o What would I look, listen, or ask for in order to know what one, a specific group, or all students are working to understand?
- • Student participation
  - o What do I want to learn about how one, a specific group, or all students participate in the learning?
  - o What specific structure(s) of participation, if any, do I want to focus attention on?
- • Curricular task and activity
  - o What would be valuable to know in terms of how one, a specific group, or all students intellectually engage in a particular task?
  - o What would help me to understand the value of a particular task or content material or a series of tasks for one, a specific group, or all students?
- • Pedagogy and practice
  - o What would I like to know about my role in structuring, facilitating, assessing, or responding to the interaction of one, a specific group, or all students with subject matter?
  - o What would help me to know the value of a specific part of my plan, or the learning theory at work in my plan, or some aspect of teaching practice in relation to my student learning goals?

    ○ Is there a particular instructional strategy or curricular approach that I am trying to incorporate into my practice? What do I want to know about my implementation?

    ○ What else would I like to understand better?

Part 2 of the Teacher Round Protocol: The Preround Orientation

The preround orientation has three basic goals:

1. To ensure that Round partners understand the context of the Round, including any relevant perspective of the Round Teacher on curriculum, student learning, and practice

2. To inform Round partners about the planned teaching and learning

3. To prepare Round partners for their role as co-observers and co-inquirers

Round partners should leave the preround orientation with an understanding of the classroom context, in particular students' understanding of subject matter and development as academic learners; with an understanding of the planned teaching and learning and its importance; and with a clear idea of what to look, listen, or ask for and try to understand as co-observers and co-inquirers.

The preround typically follows these steps:

1. Round partners read the Round sheet.

2. The Round teacher highlights key points in each section and elaborates as needed. Round partners ask questions or make comments to ensure understanding. The Round group reviews the Round inquiry closely—what to look, listen, or ask for and try to understand—and clarifies it as needed.

3. The Round teacher explains the subject matter of the Round and engages participants briefly in learning it in order to give them a firsthand experience of what students will be doing, as appropriate.

4. The Round teacher indicates whether, how, and when Round participants may interact with students and where participants should position themselves physically in the room.

Participants gather for the preround orientation in a pre-arranged space—an empty classroom, teachers' room, cafeteria, hallway, or so on. Most prerounds take 15 to 20 or fewer minutes. Sometimes, to accommodate tight schedules, as in the case of the Rounds day at UPCS (see Chapter 5), they are shortened to 5 to 7 minutes. In other instances, the preround may occur on one day and the actual Round (classroom visit) on another.

Part 3 of the Teacher Round Protocol: The Round

Once in the classroom, Teacher Round partners take up their pre-arranged positions. In some instances, this will mean standing or sitting on the periphery of the room. In others it will mean drawing up a chair alongside a small group of students to attend closely to their work or squatting until one's "quads hurt." On different occasions or at judiciously selected moments, depending on what has been agreed upon during the preround, participants might interact with individual students or a group of students—to ask questions so as to clarify and better understand what students are thinking and doing and why.

While in the classroom Teacher Round partners use their personalization skills of listening and attending closely, and discern, inquire into, and reflect on what happens in the interplay of students, subject matter, and teacher. Because there is so much that can be learned, it may be beneficial to have two observers focus on the same group of students; they will be able to combine and corroborate their observations, and they can learn from the discrepancies and differences in interpretation that inevitably arise.

Recording observations

Round partners may want to agree ahead of time on how to record observations. Here are several methods which can be used individually or in some combination:

1. Use the Round questions: Often Round partners blend observations and reflective comments in the space provided on the Round sheet below each Round question. In implementing this method, partners would do well to distinguish observations and reflective comments or questions; one way is to simply bracket any commentary.

2. Use a simple two-column observation sheet: Participants head one column with "Observations" and the adjoining column

with "Reflections/Questions" (see example below). When possible, participants note when an observation connects to a particular Round question.

3. Try verbatim records: There may be benefit in having a verbatim record of short segments (1 to 2 minutes) of any student-student or student-teacher dialogue or individual student work, coupling these with brief reflective notes in the margins or with the two-column format. In fact, during the preround orientation the Round teacher might single out a particularly important segment of a planned small or large group discussion to try to record.

Part 4 of the Teacher Round Protocol: The Postround Reflection

There are several broad principles to keep in mind during postround conversation.

- *Focus on practicable knowledge:* stay focused on understanding teaching-learning and developing practicable knowledge, that is, knowledge that can be applied to practice.
- *Describe rather than evaluate:* use observation notes to bring a concrete record of what happened to the conversation. Turn Round questions or directions on what to look and listen for, or ask students about, into statements of what you notice, see, hear, and find out ("I noticed," "I saw," "I heard," "I found out that . . .")
- *Ask questions which clarify rather than assume or imply judgment:* seek understanding of what the Round Teacher or Round partners are saying, more specifically, of the teaching-learning.
- *Reflect rather than react or prescribe:* questions which begin with "What if . . . ?" or "What would you think about [the following idea] . . . ?" and statements which begin with "I wonder if. . . ." help foster reflective discussion and open up for consideration new possibilities relative to the teaching-learning observed during the Round and for practice more generally.

The Round teacher begins the postround reflection. Because the timeframe is usually about 20 minutes or so, and there is much to try to accomplish, someone might serve the role of timekeeper if there is no facilitator or moderator. Generally, discussion proceeds through three simple phases, although groups sometimes move backwards and forwards from one to the other; I have suggested timeframes for each, but groups should adjust based on their interests and how much time overall is available.

Three phases of the postround reflection

1. First thoughts: the Round teacher's initial reflection and Round partner response

2. The inquiry: sharing and discussing observations based on the Round inquiry

3. Final reflection: What's new, what if, what next, what's left, and how did we do?

First thoughts: The Round teacher's initial reflection (2 to 4 minutes). Often, the Round teacher is eager to comment on what happened before moving explicitly to the Round inquiry. She or he may make general observations on the engagement of students, on the curricular and pedagogical approach, or on her or his actions, and invite comment. Round partners listen and respond to the Round teacher's initial observations. After a few minutes, attention turns directly to observations based on the Round inquiry, if discussion has not naturally moved in that direction already.

Inquiry: Observations based on the Round inquiry (10 to 14 minutes). The Round inquiry, the heart of the effort to learn in and from the teaching-learning, structures the main part of conversation. Each question is taken up in turn, with relevant observations and reflective comments shared by members of the group. Sometimes the observations and discussion based on one question are so rich that the other questions are set aside. This decision can be made in the moment by the Round teacher or by the Round teacher in consultation with Round partners.

Final thoughts: What's new? What if? What next? What's left? How did we do? (4 to 6 minutes). The group wraps up by reflecting on what they have learned and the implications for teaching and learning, asking some or all of the following questions:

- *What's new?* What have we learned, what are our takeaways? The "What's new?" question opens the door for Round partners to summarize specific ideas about curriculum and practice or specific insights about teaching-learning that the Teacher Round has caused them to newly consider or revisit.

- *What if?* What might we have done differently and why? The "What if?" question spurs thinking about alternative possibilities for engaging and supporting students in line with learning goals and the Round inquiry. This is usually the most challenging terrain of the postround conversation. The key question for Round partners is how to suggest an alternative that makes sense in light of shared evidence of what happened and the learning goals; that is, to build a plausible pedagogical case for what might in some way support one or more students in learning for everyone to consider thoughtfully and respectfully ("Reflecting on what we noticed in this instance, I wonder if. . . ."). This approach helps keep the focus on teaching-learning and not the Round teacher. It is a good idea to provide the Round teacher with the first opportunity to pose a "What if . . . ?" question.
- *What next?* What might we try next in order to support these students' learning and why? The Round teacher typically sketches plans for the following day(s) in light of more long-term goals and knowledge of how students are developing academically and discusses what modifications, if any, she or he might make based on the Round experience. Round participants clarify, comment, or suggest.
- *What's left?* What old or new questions about curriculum, teaching, and learning are we pondering and how might we address them?
- *How did we do?* Round partners reflect on any or all of the following: how well they did in observing, sharing observations, meeting the goals of the Round inquiry; discussing and learning about practice together during the postround reflection; and fulfilling other group norms or the group's Teacher Round compact, if there is one.

Typically, the postround reflection ends with Round partners giving their written notes to the Round Teacher.

Part 5 of the Teacher Round Protocol (Optional): Teacher Round Follow-Up

What happens after the postround reflection? A Teacher Round may be illuminating and informing for all concerned. Each participant leaves with his or her specific takeaways. Less tangible but no less important, each has had an opportunity to hone pedagogical faculties of observation and inquiry as well professional qualities of collaboration and reflection, to consider her or his own knowledge and practice repertoire, and in some measure to build common understanding of teaching and learning with colleagues.

Whether the experience of the Teacher Round is harnessed in any further way depends on its specific purposes and its relationship with other learning—in teacher teams (grade level, vertical, or some other configuration), in study groups, in preservice cohort groups, or schoolwide. Here are a few examples of what might happen:

- The teacher induction coach meets individually with the Round teacher to discuss the learning of the Teacher Round in relation to short-term teaching goals.
- The Round teacher prepares samples of student work from the Round for close examination during the Round group's weekly team meeting.
- At a weekly meeting of the Round group, teachers discuss the implications of what they have learned during the Teacher Round for their instructional priorities and curriculum planning and set mutual goals, to be reflected in Teacher Rounds planned by the group in coming months.
- At their periodic team meeting, teachers in the Round group preview each other's Teacher Rounds, based on shared instructional priorities.
- In a preservice program, the Round teacher gathers with colleagues in a practice workshop, fully prepared to examine with the group a segment of videotape from the Round as well as samples of student work generated during the Round, using protocols for this purpose.

The Teacher Round Protocol in Action: Kate's 7th Grade Mathematics Teacher Round

Kate is a veteran middle school mathematics teacher in a small urban public school. She prepared a Teacher Round for fellow math teachers and several preservice teachers. For the preservice teachers, her Teacher Round is part of an extensive process of learning about mathematics teaching and learning in a university course and in classrooms; for her colleagues, it is part of an ongoing process of sharing and developing practice together (Del Prete, 2010).

As in all of her reflective planning, Kate strives to put into action several ideas about teaching and learning that she shares with her math colleagues:

- Use a threshold problem or investigation that represents the mathematical concept well, that is accessible and solvable in different ways to accommodate students' different potential paths to understanding, and that will engage students in the thinking which underlies the concept.
- Provide frequent opportunities for students to express their thinking, including their puzzlements, through talking, writing, and demonstrating (for example, by using manipulatives).
- Give students what they need to figure things out on their own and with each other (that is, work in the sweet spot of practice).
- Support all students as mathematical thinkers, problem solvers, and members of a thinking classroom community.

Any or all of these topics—key indicators of Kate's philosophy and practice—might lend themselves to discussion during the preround orientation.

Kate's Round sheet is represented in Figure 2.1. I have edited it lightly, with Kate's permission, for the sake of space and also in light of clarifying comments Kate made in the preround conversation. I have included notes from Kate's original detailed lesson plan in Figure 2.2. These notes represent the structure and scaffolding of the lesson that Kate discussed with members of the Round group; they will make the Round sheet more understandable and give a sense of what members of the Round group understood upon entering Kate's classroom.

Kate's lesson is designed to help students transition from arithmetic to algebraic thinking and to prepare them for their study of functions. You will note that her students will encounter the Banquet Table problem as the threshold for the day's thinking. The Banquet Table problem is well-matched, in Kate's experience, to her curricular and pedagogical principles and to her goal to nurture students' algebraic thinking. You should also see a strong correspondence between Kate's Round questions and her pedagogical concerns and learning goals. Finally, note that Kate's Round inquiry includes instructions on what to look for. This is typical of Kate, who is always keen to find out whether each student is engaged, supported and integrated into learning, and one way to harness the eyes and ears of the Round group as part of the Round inquiry.

Figure 2.1 Kate's Round Sheet

Background: You will see a 7th grade math class. Students are currently beginning a patterns and functions unit to begin to lay the foundation for algebra. As we are well into spring (April), students are used to the routines, procedures, and expectations; we know each other very well.

Today we will begin one of my favorite problems (which can be solved in various ways). The "banquet table" problem has become a vital part of my curriculum. I find that it lays the foundation for many algebraic concepts and skills. I also find it important because all students, regardless of their background and mathematical expertise, can learn during the investigation. All students can count and think; therefore, all students can participate in the mathematics involved in this lesson.

Round Learning Focus: My main goal is to build students' confidence in accomplishing a mathematical task and to enable them to:

- investigate patterns;
- create algebraic rules to describe a functional relationship;
- begin to connect problem situations, diagrams, tables, rules and graphs; and
- write and interpret algebraic formulas like $y=4x+2$ or $y=(s-2)x+2$ and show an understanding of the mathematical notation.

Below, I also have listed bonus material for this lesson. I do not expect students to fully understand the following, but the lesson serves as a preview of these coming attractions:

- Equivalent algebraic expressions and the need for simplifying expressions
- Slope as the first difference and steepness of the graphed line
- Y-intercept as the constant in a situation/equation and as the point of the line that lies on the y axis
- Writing rules with more than two variables (Writing a general formula for any "s"-sided polygon and "t" number of tables.)

I would like the Round to focus on how students are working together to problem solve, develop an understanding of functional relationships, and write algebraic rules to describe a pattern and situation.

Practice focus: The success of this activity relies heavily on how I conduct the whole class discussions. Please focus on my questioning as well (See Round Question #3).

Round Inquiry

1. Are all students able to safely engage in this problem and learn some mathematics (notice mathematical patterns)? Explain what you observe that applies to this question.

2. Please record quotes or occurrences that demonstrate how students are learning from one another.

3. During whole class discussion, are students listening to one another? Am I asking questions that encourage students to share and explain their thinking? Are students' various methods for solving the problem explained fully? What signs are there that students understand the discussion?

4. What indications are there that students are thinking algebraically, in terms of a function rather than counting? Which students, if any, rely exclusively on counting, even when asked to calculate the number of tables needed for any number of guests? What do you notice about their ways of figuring out the problem or their response to other students' algebraic thinking? How might they be supported?

Figure 2.2 Notes From Kate's Lesson Plan

Classwork design: Students will be seated in assigned groups of three, as they often are. For this task, students generally will be in mixed-ability groups. Throughout the class, I will pose a scenario and a question to students. I will expect them to first think independently. Then, they will be encouraged to share their thinking with their group members before I summon a whole class discussion on various ways used to answer the question asked. Another question will be posed and the cycle will be repeated.

Entry problem: To begin our investigation, I will describe the scenario of having to prepare banquet tables for an undetermined number of guests. The function coordinator determines the number of people he or she can let into the banquet based on the number of tables the unreliable table inputter has set up. Based on the number of tables prepared, students need to determine the number of seats. This situation serves as a model for a functional relationship in that the number of people relies directly on the number of tables.

Discovering patterns: To determine the number of seats, students will create a table with a column for the number of banquet tables and a second column for the number of seats and look for a pattern. Students will find the number of people who can sit at 1, 2, 3, and 4 square tables. I will provide visuals and manipulatives representing the tables and how they are arranged. Here is a drawing of 5 square tables. The tables must be assembled like so:

Supporting formula development and sharing: Once they have looked for and described patterns in their two-column tables, students will be asked to find the number of people who can sit at 10 and 100 tables. This jump is vital in trying to find an algebraic rule so that students look for a quick trick instead of simply extending the table. Once students have individually developed a method for finding the number of people who can sit at 100 tables, they will be asked to describe their method in words—to write down their thinking. Students will then be able to communicate their individual methods within their small groups; then we will discuss the various methods as a whole class.

Generalizing: Before students are able to write a rule in algebraic form for a situation, most first need to articulate the rule in words. For this reason, I will ask students to write a letter to the new hire who will be in charge of determining how many people can be admitted to the banquet hall based on any number of tables prepared. This is the first time students will be asked to generalize and describe a method for any number (not just 1, 2, 3, 4, 10, and 100). In this letter, students will be encouraged to include a formula for finding the number of people based on the number of tables. Again, students need to work individually and then may discuss their letters in small groups.

Whole class sharing and formula writing: Students will then be asked to share their letters, methods, and formulas with the class. This class discussion will be very important

(Continued)

Figure 2.2 (Continued)

> to the success of the activity, as it will involve discussing various methods. It's my hope that all students' methods are validated and understood by others.
>
>   Written dialogues: Students may rewrite or add to their letter to the function coordinator after the discussions take place. I, as the function coordinator, will write back to the students after their final submission and ask for any needed clarification. Students and I will converse back and forth through writing, if necessary, until they show understanding of their method, informally and algebraically.

Kate's Preround Orientation

Kate's Round partners begin by reviewing her Round sheet. Kate highlights her goals, stressing how important it is, in her view, for students to gain confidence in themselves as mathematical thinkers, recognize that everyone's thoughts have value in the learning process, and to grow accustomed to talking and writing about their thinking. For many of her students, although they have had Kate already for a year as their teacher, math is an intimidating subject; many are afraid of math. So revisiting and reestablishing learning norms which build participation and confidence is as important for Kate as the development of algebraic understanding; one will benefit the other in the long run.

Kate talks about how she is putting her teaching philosophy into action. Essentially reviewing the phases of the learning activity (as reflected in the notes from her lesson provided above), she explains how the combination of individual work (including students' written accounts of their reasoning), small group sharing of individual solutions, and whole class discussion is calculated to affirm and make visible different ways of thinking, leading to the possibility of a student-constructed rule (a function) that can solve the problem for any number of tables. The group talks briefly with Kate about the attributes of the problem that help create accessibility and encourage algebraic thinking. Everyone can count and think and notice things— including the number patterns that emerge in the course of solving the problem—so, as Kate will remind students, they can do math.

The group pauses for a few minutes to try the banquet table problem individually and then together.

They generate several different ways to think through the problem in order to prepare themselves to recognize some of the different ways they might see students use in the classroom. This leads to a review of what they will look and listen for during the individual, small group, and whole class phases to indicate the development of different students' thinking and address Kate's Round inquiry. Each Round member will sit near one of the groups of three students.

Kate's Round

I have provided a sample of notes that I took during Kate's Round, using the two column approach, in Figure 2.3. I've added clarifying words to my original scrawled notes, as needed. I've included only a few short segments of notes for purposes of illustration; an ellipsis (. . .) indicates the gap between different segments.

Figure 2.3   Observation Notes from Kate's Round

Key Round question: What indications are there that students are thinking algebraically, in terms of a function rather than counting?	
Observation Notes	*Reflections/Questions*
T (Teacher): "Find the # of seats for 3, 4, and 5 tables then do a 'jump' to 10. No talking—silent thinking time right now."	The "jump" encourages algebraic thinking
S-A (Student A): Uses chart paper and draws individual tables. Explains: "For every single [added] table add 2 more people—4, 6, 8, 10, 12, jump 22. This is how I figured out how to fill in the blanks [in his table]."	Is he adding in his head or using a "rule?"
Teacher asks whole class for "different methods" of figuring out	Explain "methods"; everyone has some method—everyone is included; makes thinking visible
S-B: "[I] counted around the edges [of the tables]...found the perimeter of tables which was 12. For 5 [tables], 5×2 + 2."	Is there any relationship between "adding" around the perimeter and determining a functional relationship?
T: "Figure out how many people for 100 tables. Write a letter about how to find the number of people at any given # of tables. See if you can include 'a rule.'" [silent thinking time]	Writing their thinking about a rule (work out functional relationship)
S-C: 100 tables [will seat] 220 people. T: "Let me see if I understand...It makes sense to me...Does it make sense? Why not? Think about it."	She uses multiplication (if 10 tables = 22, then 100 = 10× 22 or 220)? Ask for more explanation of her thinking? What if she compares her thinking to others?
S-D offers a "rule": 4 (seats) × n (number of tables) minus # of "gaps" [the edges of tables that are together] × 2...	Example of reasoning that shows understanding of a functional relationship

The observations in Figure 2.3 point to potential contributions I might make as a reflective observer to the postround conversation. I am able to give examples of different students' thinking (Students A, B, C, and D). Apropos the Round questions, I am able to distinguish students who figure out a solution using simple math (e.g., counting) and those who figure out a functional relationship and rule for any solution, or who do both. I am also curious about Student C's thinking (circled in the notes in Figure 2.3) and how to respond to it: what would happen if she revisited her thinking verbally or compared it to the thinking of other students? What happens when she writes an explanation of her rule? I can help address the question of what happens to the thinking of students who start out using counting or simple math during the class—whether and how they come to understand the possibility of a rule. On this basis, I might also contribute to a conversation about the curricular task and how the curriculum might unfold so as to continue the development of students' understanding of functional relationships.

As the excerpts from my notes suggest, the Round is a treasure trove of examples of student engagement and thinking. This richness is due in no small measure to the structure of the lesson and student participation, the accessibility of the threshold task, the ways Kate, who has dedicated herself to this way of teaching, draws out and makes student thinking visible and comprehensible, and the extent to which the exchange of different ideas has become a norm of learning for these students. In a sense, Kate has not only created ample opportunity to migrate into the minds of her learners, she has opened up and drawn out their minds as an integral part of the whole class's learning. In so doing, she has put herself in a stronger position to follow students' thinking so that she might figure out how best to lead them. In this way, she also has made more visible her own effort to personalize and respond to student thinking—in other words, her adaptive expertise—for members of the Teacher Round group. There is plenty to talk about during the postround reflection.

Postround Reflection

First thoughts: Kate's initial comments are strongly student focused. She speaks positively of the engagement of students and the extent of participation and then gets more detailed. She points out examples of the patterns students discovered in their two-column tables showing the number of seats (second column) next to the number of banquet tables (first column), including the fact that the number of seats increases by 2 for each additional table. Kate also identifies different methods students used to jump to 10 tables and then 100; less clear is whether all students understand the different methods in every case. Round participants add examples to Kate's.

Inquiry: The bulk of discussion centers on Round questions 3 and 4 regarding the thinking of students individually, in their groups of three, and in whole class discussion. Round colleagues point out instances of students counting the seats around tables, using manipulatives, or drawing their own visual models. There are also examples of students who start with this method and who then try more efficient ones. For example, Kate mentions students who used a counting method—counting the seats one-by-one—and who then determined "a functional relationship involving multiplying by 2 and adding 2." We note as well students who stop counting using a visual model of the banquet tables when they notice in their two–column tables that there are two additional seats for each additional table; they add two seats for each additional table rather than count up the seats for all of the tables, even when they have to jump to 10 tables. Then, rather than try to add up seats, they begin to search for a rule when they have to determine the number of seats at 100 tables. Student C in my notes is a prime example of a student developing a rule that does not work; a pivotal question in the postround is how to respond in a situation such as this one.

We talk about Student C, who was so confident in her calculation that there are 220 seats available at 100 tables. This is a poignant moment in the postround. Kate reflects on her response, which was to ask Student C "to think about it." She might have stayed with the student in the moment—attended a little more closely—in order to learn the root of her idea: what was her rule and why? Both the student and her peers might have benefited if Kate had asked her to explain, had drawn out her thinking further. Kate laments having lost what she views as a teachable moment. But we note that Kate did double back to Student C late in the class, to discover that her erroneous rule was an extrapolation of her answer for 10 tables—if 10 tables provide 22 seats, then 100 tables must provide 10 times that amount (since $10 \times 10 = 100$) or 220 seats. Finding out, as it were, the mind of Student C, Kate was prompted to ask other students to explain how they arrived at their answers for 100 tables. "Why does it make sense to do $100 \times 2 + 2$?" Kate asks students at one point. And then, "Is anybody else confused?" Kate explains that she relied on student thinking at variance with that of Student C to help Student C rethink her own approach; she enlisted peers, in effect, to become Student C's thought partners.

Final thoughts: What's new, what if, what next, what's left, and how did we do? What's new (takeaways)? There is some discussion of the structure of Kate's lesson, how it supported different learners, and how it enabled Kate to personalize her support. There is discussion, in addition, of how students come to the idea of a rule or function. For some students counting seats (around the perimeter of a visual image of the tables) or noting patterns in their two-column tables prove important interim steps toward developing a clear function. Providing opportunity for students to take these interim steps— knowing, as a matter of a teacher's effort to work in a zone of optimal learning, that this is part of the process of students figuring out a rule on their own—is a central lesson. The group wonders how many students actually formed a rule—a workable function— in this manner.

What if? Kate's work with Student C becomes emblematic of the dynamic between individual and whole group learning and how a teacher facilitates it. The group wonders about alternatives in the moment, leading to a "what if?" question: what if Kate had asked Student C whether she could explain her answer by using a visual representation of the tables? Might that have caused Student C to rethink her approach just as well as the strategy of having her listen to the ideas of others?

What's left: Kate mentions the importance of the students' letters to the function coordinator, giving their advice about how to figure out the number of seats available. The letters will give Kate an important glimpse into the mind of each student and each student's learning. Some, such as the example in Figure 2.4, will result in a clarifying exchange with Kate, the function coordinator.

Next steps for Kate include learning from the students' letters. She also plans a more advanced version of the banquet table problem for the following day: "Students will investigate what happens when the tables are different shapes. They will do the same steps as [today] . . . they will use manipulatives and visuals and see many patterns. . . they will be encouraged to find a general rule for any sided polygon." Kate will again ask students to look at patterns in two-column tables and graphs they will produce. By asking students simply "What do you notice?" she hopes students will see patterns that lead to informal discussion of slope and y-intercept. She will again rely on written letters from students "as an assessment and learning tool."

There is no time for reflection on the Teacher Round learning process. The Teacher Round ends with group members having had

Figure 2.4   Sample of a Student's Exchange With the "Function Coordinator"

Dear Function Coordinator,

A method you can use to find how many people sit at any number of tables is you can add 1 to the number of tables then multiply that by 2. For example if there are 100 tables you would add 1 because

100

1   [   ]   1

100

  of the 1 person at the end so $(100 + 1) \times 2$. You multiply it by 2 because on the other side there's 100 and 1 person at the end. I hope I was a help.

***

Dear ___,

That definitely helps me. I am guessing that for any number you add one and multiply the sum by two. Is that correct? If that is true, can a formula be written? Please write back. Thanks.

The Function Coordinator

***

Dear Function Coordinator,

A formula you can use is $(n+1) \times 2$. N stands for number of tables. You add 1 because of the one person at the end, then you multiply that by 2 because of the both sides. . . .

---

an opportunity to think in detail about mathematical learning, teaching that personalizes, and the classroom as a thinking community.

Round Follow-Up

For Kate and her colleagues, the Round is part of an ongoing collaboration, in regular team meetings, dedicated to understanding how to cultivate the mathematical confidence and capabilities of students from one year to the next; and, also, how to actualize the values, instructional framework, and college readiness goals they share in common with all teachers in their school. For the preservice teachers, Kate's Round is one of many they have participated in over the course of the school year, including their own; it is integrated into an ongoing process of collaborative learning, developing their own practice, and reflection (see Appendix B).

The following chapters help to prepare you further to use the Teacher Round protocol, to visualize the process, and to consider its potential for learning. The next two chapters provide detailed examples of Teacher Round learning at the secondary and elementary levels. Chapter 5 describes a full Rounds day at Kate's school and illustrates the potential impact of the learning process at this scale. Chapter 6 provides a more in-depth look at key parts of the Teacher Round process: inquiry, observation, and reflective conversation. Appendix C provides a streamlined outline of the Teacher Round protocol as it was introduced at one school.

3

Teacher Round Learning in High School

This chapter contains detailed examples of Teacher Round learning at the high school level. Much of what is illustrated and explained in these examples, however, is relevant to Teacher Round learning at any level. The examples include Teacher Rounds conducted by teachers for colleagues and teacher interns, and Teacher Rounds hosted by teacher interns themselves. They represent different disciplines at the high school level—English, physics, visual art, and history.

Leann's Teacher Round, in English, appears first. Her Teacher Round was one of two consecutive weekly sessions that she hosted for colleagues and secondary English teacher interns. It reflects a teacher grappling with the challenge of cultivating her students' intellectual risk-taking and analytical capabilities. Tara, a physics teacher intent on joining together hands-on and conceptual learning, also conducted a Teacher Round for colleagues and teacher interns. Phoebe and Jeremy S., both teacher interns, host Teacher Rounds in visual art and history respectively; each is working out the basics of a pedagogy which engages all students fully in learning that is consistent with the norms of learning in their disciplines. The chapter concludes with a brief summary of a preround orientation led by a different Jeremy. It suggests the kind of rich discussion that can transpire in clarifying a teacher's purpose and approach—in this particular case, a creative effort to integrate content understanding and pedagogy.

In terms of setting, the two Jeremys taught at University Park Campus School (UPCS), a small, high performing urban school (see Chapter 5). Leann, Tara, and Phoebe were teaching at South High School. In contrast to UPCS, South High is large and functioned for a long time as a comprehensive high school with an uncontested tradition of tracking. For more than a decade, South High administrators and teachers have strived to implement a curriculum which prepares all students for postsecondary education. In its physical design, South High is unusual. It has few floor-to-ceiling walls, a feature which most who teach there would gladly change; the open spaces often reverberate with what is, for most first-time visitors, a distracting cacophony. Demographically, UPCS and South High are similar, with comparably high percentages of students qualifying for free or reduced lunch (over 80%) or considered nonnative speakers (about 60%).

The learning reflected in these Teacher Round examples is but a small window opening onto an expansive and varied landscape, one in which teachers work everyday, yet one underexplored, and often underappreciated and misapprehended. Although a small sample, they should suggest the insistent and engaging complexity of practice at mature as well as beginning levels of development—the problems and pedagogical challenges that can be confronted, the rich and informing detail that it is possible to uncover in a single episode of classroom learning, the compelling moments of student effort that easily get overlooked without eyes and ears to see and hear and learn from them, and the layers of inquiry and reflection that open to greater understanding and possibility. They should help illustrate what can be gained, in terms of a teacher's knowledge and practice repertoire and adaptive expertise, from openly and inquiringly entering one's intricate world of teaching and learning with others.

Leann's Teacher Round: Understanding Theme in English Literature

Overview

Leann is intent on expanding her students' understanding of theme. Her students often mistake a topic in a piece of literature for

its thematic message. She wants them to move beyond this simplifi-
cation to a more analytical understanding. Adding to her challenge,
her particular group of students has shown reluctance to venture
intellectually. On the one hand, they play it safe, concerned for getting
the right answer and for grades; on the other, they lack confidence
and experience as inquiring thinkers. She feels challenged by the fact
that these students are in an AP Literature course in which facility
with literary analysis is essential. At the same time, many students
have not experienced an AP course before, and she wants to support
them to achieve at a level that is higher than what has been expected
of them—and what perhaps they have expected of themselves—in
the past.

Leann's first step is to choose content worthy of her goal. To com-
plicate and develop her students' notion of theme, she has chosen a
set of readings which treat the idea of love in different ways. Her next
challenge is to define ways to engage students to probe the readings
and uncover the meanings of love embedded in them. Then she must
help students articulate the thematic ideas and show how the text
supports their interpretation. Much of the postround reflection
focuses on the effectiveness of the scaffolding she uses to meet these
challenges.

Round Partners

At the time of her Teacher Round, Leann is a "teacher fellow" in
the university-school partnership, teaching two classes at her high
school and otherwise serving as a mentor for a cohort group of
teacher interns teaching English in her building. Her Teacher
Rounds are planned in conjunction with a course on teaching in
the humanities. Her Round partners include the course instructor,
several colleagues, and a half dozen teacher interns. The Teacher
Rounds set in relief Leann's discipline-based pedagogical thinking,
her reflection on a typical challenge of practice, and her commitment
to learn collaboratively.

Preround Orientation

Leann emphasizes that "theme is complicated," that her students
"struggle with theme and meaning" and how meaning is established, and that she wants them to understand and work within the
complexity. It is still early in the year, and she is working through
how to open students to less cautious, more probing and authentic

Figure 3.1 Leann's Round Sheet

Background: This is a 12th grade AP English Lit class . . . Overall these kids are very willing to discuss, highly motivated by grades, happy with constant feedback and an understanding of what the class's objectives are, and a bit unwilling to take risks with their ideas about literature—they often stick to more clichéd and bland interpretations of texts, something I am hoping to change as the year goes on.

This class is the beginning of a week and a half . . . in which we read short stories and analyze important literary techniques in these stories that contribute to meaning. This is connected with my efforts to get the class functioning in what I call "AP thinking"—reading literature with attention to strong analysis of overall meaning and, importantly, strong analysis of how the author achieves this meaning. Generally I find—and these students are no exception—that my seniors come up with themes that are fairly clichéd and have trouble going beyond just identifying literary techniques and trying to figure out what these techniques are actually doing.

Learning Focus: The objective of this lesson is to help students recognize how techniques like setting, symbolism, and especially characterization can help contribute to our understanding of the overall meaning of a story. Moreover, I am hoping they will see how constructing the meaning of a story, the big themes, is a thinking, messy process—not a process of just fitting a moral of the story into a nice little sentence.

We will [start with] two love poems by Pablo Neruda, in which students will be asked to share their thoughts on the themes of the poem and the lines that help them recognize that theme. This is to get them thinking in the mode of identifying theme and going into the text to support it.

From here, we will delve into the short story they read over the weekend, beginning with some discussion about meaning and reader responses. Students will be asked to share in groups their thoughts on theme and how setting and symbol help create theme. We will act out the story and students will be asked to identify certain moments of characterization that they think really help contribute to the theme.

The class will end with Exit Slips . . . the students will be asked to construct a potential thesis for a paper that asks them to consider how this author uses characterization.

Round Inquiry

1. Does the exercise with the Neruda poems seem worthwhile in getting students thinking about the themes around love in literature and to see the value of looking closely at a few moments in a text? Is it useful in scaffolding the work with the short story—what evidence is there to show that the learning from one informs the other?

2. I'm always unsure about the value of reading out loud to certain classes—does the reading of the characters' dialogue seem useful to the class, especially in recognizing characterization? What evidence of usefulness do you see?

3. I want my students to see that it is hard to construct meaning, and that it just doesn't come to us in a simple prepackaged sentence. But does it seem like my allowing them to work through their ideas about theme out loud in class makes the question of theme more confusing?

discussion—to promote literary discussion and at the same time create a culture of trust and risk-taking conducive to it. Consistent with Leann's Round questions, the Round group will focus its observation on the development of student ideas about the theme of love in the readings and whether the structure and tasks of the lesson support their thinking.

Leann's Round questions touch directly on her choice of subject matter, student tasks, and the learning theory underlying the lesson. She wonders about her choice of literary examples—in particular Neruda's poems ("Leaning Into the Afternoons" and "Sonnet XXVIII")—vis-à-vis her goal to open up the concept of theme. Do the poems lend themselves to considering some of the beauty and complexity of love, to moving beyond the idea of *love* as theme to something with more warp and weft? Will discussion of the poems prepare the way for an understanding of theme in literature?

The Round

During the actual Round, students talk to each other about what meaning they see in the poems and what lines support the meaning. In large group discussion, two students build the idea that "love and beauty . . . will prevail" from a reference to the text. Students think and venture in a way that Leann hopes for, but the process is slow and uncertain. After discussion of the poems, her question prompts nudge students to explore the meaning of love in the story "Love in L.A." "Is *love* a theme? Is "Love in L.A." a love story?" The story is by no means a version of the typical boy-meets-girl-and-falls-in-love story and Leann hopes it causes examination of what "love story" can mean. Again students stutter through some possibilities. Leann scaffolds discussion by asking students to identify setting, symbol, and characterization and how they shed light on the idea of *love* in "Love in L.A."

Her second Round question focuses on her strategy of reading dialogue out loud as a way to highlight the process of characterization. Two students, a girl and boy, volunteer to read a section of dialogue from the short story while Leann fills in the narrator's voice. The act of trying to represent the character's voices forces all of the students to listen afresh to the characters. The calculated evasiveness and cavalier attitude of the male character comes through loudly; so does his moment of surprised introspection as he shakes the woman's hand. Student comments afterward reflect these dimensions of the character. On the one hand, the male character is "fake" and "sly" and, on the other, is "proud and sad about his performance." This last comment intrigues Leann, who responds, "You're getting at his potential for love." The students are responding to the male character's reaction to the touch of the girl's hand as they shake, and Leann coaxes them to consider the meaning of this moment.

Postround Reflection

One or two members of the Teacher Round group wonder whether the dramatic reading of the story served the purpose of re-engaging students. Another wonders about the potential value of asking students to write down their thoughts about characterization while listening. And so this particular way of engaging students in the story—the scaffolding that is at the heart of Leann's pedagogy—gets constructive attention.

The largest chunk of postround discussion probes Leann's concern, as reflected in her third Round question, for whether the lesson uncovers the complexity of theme without causing too much confusion. Members of the Round group note that Leann's students talked among themselves at two different points during the lesson to clarify what they saw as theme, that students considered ideas about love beyond the conventional, and that they used evidence from their texts to support ideas. The Round group concludes generally that the "messiness" that Leann anticipated, and that she postulates is important for getting them to take risks and "think at a higher level," was a worthwhile part of the learning process. This is important validation for Leann, as she builds her practice to support literary inquiry linked to theme. The Teacher Round gives general support to a learning process that hovers for a time in a thinking space determined by boundaries, hopes, and supports for literary discussion and the emergence and development of student ideas and analytical confidence. And, adding to her knowledge repertoire and adaptive expertise, Leann leaves with ideas, such as using writing as a tool to aid students' examination, to inform her scaffolding next time. The Round group, for its part, benefits from the example of her open and reflective questioning and her practice.

Follow-Up

In her Teacher Round a week later, Leann continues the class exploration of love as theme. Students in small groups work to identify what different literary devices—characterization, tone, symbolism, and point of view—disclose about love in the short story, "Summer," by David Updike. Leann charges students with figuring out how Updike uses a particular literary device "to convey meaning." This task and the group work form the thinking space and the learning process. Leann puts herself inside this space to "encourage and assist students." Her core Round question, aimed at the sweet spot of teaching and learning, is: "Does my help seem to remain 'help' and not answers? Do the students still seem to be coming up with their analysis and evaluation on their own?" She also asks, "Is there a way to make this more productive?"

In a group discussing characterization, one student comments, "Maybe this goes against the convention that love is always worth fighting for . . . Love is not always worth fighting for, at least not without a worthy cause." Another group develops the idea that "Updike uses season (summer) to mirror inevitable changes of adolescence." These are signs of the kind of probing for which Leann hopes. But Round observers note that some students "play it safe" or are still learning to respond to each other, to pay attention to and build on each other's ideas. At this early point in students' development as group as well as literary learners, Leann must make it difficult for groups to play it safe rather than delve into complex ideas through close examination of the text. A suggestion to help her meet this challenge emerges in the postround, as one Round member wonders whether group work might be structured in stages so that students individually write down and share ideas about the use of a literary device and repeat this process to address how a device conveys meaning. Once again, the Teacher Round process delves into purpose and scaffolding and responds to Leann's effort to cultivate literary understanding of theme in tandem with analytical confidence and capability. Overall, Leann's two Teacher Rounds, centered on the same complex problem of practice, helped her to assess and refine teaching and learning in her class.

Questions of Practice

At the heart of Leann's Round lesson lies a core question of disciplinary learning—how to foster a complex literary discussion based on the idea of theme? This question draws out critical interlinked dimensions of practice—content, curriculum, pedagogy, and context (in particular, her students and their school). What literary materials will serve the purpose? How to promote literary discussion with a group of students who delve into complexity reluctantly at best, who try to identify the answer they think the teacher is expecting more than trust and rely on their own honest thinking? How to open up the concept of theme?

Closely related, Leann is trying to move students from an information-gathering mode of interacting with the text to an inquiring and analytical one. How to move students from identifying a literary technique to analysis of what purpose the technique serves—to move them beyond searching for examples of literary elements to literary analysis and searching for meaning?

Leann's lesson also confronts a curriculum issue that will be familiar to many teachers. She feels tension between the imperatives of an AP class and the imperative to teach so as to meet the needs demonstrated by her students. How to accommodate the fast pace of a prescribed curriculum with the slower more calibrated pace of learning that particular students may need to achieve curricular goals?

Leann's Teacher Rounds address these questions constructively but do not answer them definitively. They do give support for the kind of structured and purposeful "messiness" for which she plans and for the extended investigation of a single theme (love), using various literary pieces, in meeting her goal to promote more analytical inquiry. They point more generally to the provisional nature of teaching, to the constant interplay of the different kinds of knowledge that comprise a teacher's repertoire and adaptive expertise—personal knowledge about beliefs, relational knowledge about students and their learning, knowledge about curriculum and learning goals, and knowledge about pedagogy and academic discipline—as she determines how to keep each student in an optimal zone of learning.

Tara's Teacher Round: Investigating Free Fall in One Dimension

Overview

Tara's physics class is heterogeneous. In addition to reflecting the rich cultural and linguistic diversity of South High, students come from different grade levels (11th and 12th) and vary in their academic performance. Tara wants them to figure out for themselves "that all objects fall with a constant acceleration if air resistance is ignored." She also plans for them to apply kinematics equations to determine what is happening to an object in free fall in terms of time, its rate of speed, or distance traveled. She expects as well that her students will exercise habits of scientific learning—observing, testing ideas, and interpreting and using physical evidence accurately—and further develop as a community of scientific learners.

Free fall is a terrific topic from the point of view of everyday experience and physics. Everyone is intimately familiar with the phenomenon of falling, yet there are different views about what happens and why. Tara's students have a mix of formal and intuitive knowledge to bring to the discussion, having already investigated speed and acceleration. In creating a space for optimal learning, Tara must take into account students' preconceptions about how objects fall and why.

Tara structures the day's lesson in several parts. During "bell work" (the work that typically starts the class) students will write down their answers to questions based on several free-fall scenarios (see Tara's Round Sheet on page 52). After forming their ideas they will share and discuss them in small groups—a process to which they have become accustomed over the past few weeks—and clarify them in the whole group. Then they will observe enactments of several of the scenarios. Repeating the pattern of small and whole group discussion, they will compare the observed evidence with their preconceptions, share their ideas, and work together to develop a common explanation for what they saw.

Tara's lesson rests on a three-part theory of learning: that the opportunity for students to examine their own ideas about the behavior of falling objects will encourage inquiry; that asking students to test their ideas against real physical evidence is a powerful way to help them develop understanding; and that the process of sharing, comparing, and building on one another's ideas and interpretations of the physical evidence will further support the development of understanding and habits of scientific learning.

Round Partners

Tara's Round partners include several colleagues and teacher interns who are beginning to teach science at the high school level, including a mentor from the university who supports the teacher interns and who participates with Tara and her colleagues on a team of science teachers dedicated to sharing and developing their practice.

Preround Orientation

As Tara concludes her explanation of the lesson and her Round questions in the preround orientation, one of her Round partners asks how she will draw on students' preconceived notions about falling

Figure 3.2 Tara's Round Sheet

Background: In the current unit we have been developing ways to describe motion. So far we have looked at motion with a constant velocity and motion with constant acceleration in one dimension. Students have been introduced to the four separate equations used to describe constant acceleration motion and have used these to solve problems. Today they will be introduced to a special case of constant acceleration, free fall. The lesson corresponds to the curriculum standard on motion and forces and math skills involving simple algebraic expressions, conversions within a unit (e.g., centimeters to meters), and use of common prefixes such as milli-, centi-, and kilo-. Assessment will occur through verbal questioning, in-class work, and homework.

Learning Focus: The goals of the lesson are to explore and address student preconceptions regarding free fall; establish that when there is no air resistance all objects fall at the same rate; and that objects, as they fall, are speeding up. On earth this rate is approximately 10 m/s^2. Students will then apply this idea to describe the motion of objects in free fall and also use the kinematics equations to solve free fall problems.
   "Bell work" (starter) questions for students:

1. A hammer and feather are dropped at the same time on the moon. Would you expect them to hit the ground at the same time? Provide a reason for your answer.

2. A flat piece of paper and a textbook are dropped in the classroom at the same time. Would you expect them to hit the ground at the same time? Provide a reason for your answer.

3. Describe the motion of a person who falls out of a hovering hot air balloon, in terms of velocity, distance covered every second, acceleration, and so on.

Round Inquiry

1. Participation: During bell work, what evidence is there that having students comment via writing first and then having small group discussion supported participation of all or most students?

2. Did the four activities spark student interest and discussion? What did you observe during this portion of the lesson? Specifically, what ideas about weight, gravity, mass, speed, and acceleration did students have? How did these ideas change, if at all, for different students during the course of the lesson? What was most challenging for students to figure out?

3. Did you see a difference in levels of participation during the white board activity (when the four cases were reviewed?)? How could that have been improved?

4. To what extent were students developing their own understanding of content?

objects. This question turns out to be critical in determining the course of the lesson. As designed, the lesson begins with students writing down their ideas about what will happen to the falling objects in the three scenarios she gives to them as "bell work." Concerned for time, Tara had planned to bypass discussion of these written ideas and move directly to the physical evidence of what happens. But the preround question causes her to reconsider the value of whole group discussion of student preconceptions.

The Round

Tara decides to invite students to share their initial ideas in response to the three "bell work" scenarios. The results are rewarding, as students generate a host of ideas and questions, and discussion heightens their curiosity. The question about what will happen when a feather and a hammer are dropped from the same height at the same time on the moon proves especially provocative. In one group of four, students wonder about the difference in gravitational pull on the moon and on earth and how the difference affects an object's falling behavior. Will an object "float around" more on the moon? One group ponders the difference between weight and mass and how one or the other might influence the action of falling. Trying to clarify the issue, one student in whole group discussion asserts that "gravity pulls weight," suggesting that gravity and weight are linked but mass is different. Another student counters that gravity might pull on mass but not weight and that the hammer has more mass, implying that it will fall faster than the feather. Drawing on his prior knowledge, a student says that on earth the difference is air resistance, and cites Galileo in claiming that they (hammer and feather) will arrive at the ground at the same time. But this introduction of an acknowledged authority fails to sway one student, who replies, "I still think it would be different because of different weight." Tara chooses not to focus on the various meanings of the terms that students use to try to explain their thinking. Instead she keeps open a space into which all students can safely bring and stand up for their various ideas and lets curiosity build. Students will have a chance to see some of their ideas put to an empirical test. This becomes the pivot point, so to speak, of the inquiry process in her class, the point at which student intrigue over whether their own ideas hold up in the physical world engages them in examining, questioning, and testing phenomena more or less closely; puts them, whether they are disposed to it or not, in a scientific frame of mind.

During the next segment of the lesson students prepare a two-column observation sheet, one column for a quick sketch of what they observe, the second for writing down observations. Attention shifts to the screen in front of the class as Tara announces that they will be going to the moon to check on the hammer/feather scenario.

Sure enough, astronaut and commander David Scott of Apollo 15 appears on screen and, in the crackling voice of lunar transmissions, says that he will test Galileo's idea with a hammer and feather. He drops them and they sink to the ground simultaneously, to the wonderment of several students. Tara follows by dropping a textbook and a piece of paper, once with the paper separate from the textbook, and once with the paper directly on top of it. A student wonders what will happen if the paper is underneath the textbook and she tries that as well.

Fervent discussion ensues in small groups, each observed by one of the Round partners. When Tara asks for summaries of group discussion (see sample notes in Figure 3.3), spokespersons state variously that the objects fall at the same rate with no resistance ("they fall at the same rate because there is no air resistance" and "with no air resistance free fall is constant" and "things fall at an equal rate unless there is a variable to affect it, such as wind resistance."). Tara comments on the use of words such as "rate" and "constant" and asks what they mean. She then diverts attention to a device in the room which imprints small dots on a strip of paper at regular intervals as it free falls. The device is activated, the resultant dotted strip of paper is passed around, and some discussion ensues as to what the spacing between the dots means. These questions will frame the next lesson.

Tara concludes by asking students to write down what they thought prior to observation and the difference between what they thought and what they saw. Their individual responses will give her an indication of how the thinking of each has developed and also whether there are lingering misconceptions and puzzlements that might be addressed next time.

Figure 3.3 Tara's Round: Sample Observation Notes

Round Observation Notes	Reflections/Questions
Student A: "With no air resistance, free fall is constant."	Meaning of speed vs. acceleration?
Student B: "Objects on the moon fall at the same rate due to lack of wind resistance regardless of weight or mass. [On] earth [it] depends on air resistance, acceleration is changing, getting faster."	Theories—trying to work out what happens in free fall—question of relationships of speed, air resistance, acceleration.
Student A: "Things fall at an equal rate unless there is a variable to affect it, such as wind resistance."	

Postround Reflection

Tara begins the postround discussion, combining her thoughts about what happened with what's next. She explains that she "asked [students] to report out their preconceptions based on the preround" discussion and that she "only got through half the lesson" to allow for more sharing. She wonders whether students might have benefited from a structured format in discussing their ideas, such as a fishbowl strategy. She also decides that she will begin the next day's class by asking students to write about something they saw that was different from what they expected—this idea prompts a brief discussion affirming the value of having students voice their puzzlements or questions from the previous day's activity. Tara also explains that she plans to videotape a falling pumpkin with students in an upcoming class (it is, after all, close to Halloween). Students will be able to time the fall and do a frame-by-frame prediction and analysis about the rate at which it is falling and what that means.

In addressing the Round inquiry, the Round group notes the interesting questions raised by students in small group discussion as they sorted through ways to understand the factors that influence falling—questions such as the difference between gravity on the moon and on earth, the effect the lunar variety of gravity has on a falling object, and the relationships among weight, mass and gravity (Do you need gravity to have weight?). Tara suggests that she might have taken "the lesson deeper" by probing students' use of these terms. It is not clear, however, that the benefits of doing so would have outweighed the benefit of staying focused on observing and discussing the fate of different falling objects. The postround group struggles for a moment with the core question of how the experience of testing and developing their personal ideas about falling can contribute to the development of students' understanding of related scientific concepts. This question bears on theories of learning and teaching science, and the group goes no farther than to voice support for the process of student inquiry and scientific thinking that has been started. Tara's plan to have students study the fall of a pumpkin, among other activities, is designed to continue the dynamic of observation, analysis, and conceptual development. As a "what if?" suggestion, one Round member wonders whether adding a "prediction" column to the observation sheet that students use will give students and Tara a record of the relationship between what students think will happen and what they see.

Teaching for the Sweet Spot in Science

This is a class designed to promote the development of understanding by observing, questioning, interpreting, and drawing conclusions from physical evidence—all important habits of scientific learning. All of these processes are evident in the lesson. Tara's Teacher Round thus offers members of the Round group an opportunity to reflect on discipline-specific pedagogical questions. Chief among them is how to take into account student preconceptions—their naïve or learned ideas—in the process of developing scientific understanding.

Tara puts her faith in the power of her students to express and develop sound ideas based on physical evidence rather than listen to her or to some other expert view. In aiming for the sweet spot of student learning, she puts a certain burden on her planning and pedagogy. How to help students examine their own ideas and move from them to understanding? She must structure opportunity for students to work through any difference between what they think must happen to falling objects and what does happen. This process of "working through" is where her pedagogical skill—her knowledge repertoire and adaptive expertise—also must focus. She relies principally on questions which ask students to think about, share, and then discuss their theories with each other both before and after they watch physical demonstrations. By asking students to write down their own thinking in relation to the physical evidence and give it to her at the end of class, she gains additional information on the state of student understanding to inform her planning.

In this particular class, small group discussions produce a consistent set of conclusions for what the physical evidence means. In the process, students grapple with concepts such as weight, gravity, rate of falling, constant acceleration, and air resistance, and these become concepts for further exploration and clarification later on. The lesson in this sense is generative—it brings forth questions and ideas that Tara would like students to pursue on the way to developing both conceptual and mathematical understanding of the phenomenon of falling. It supports a process of scientific learning.

Much of Tara's planning and assessment is focused on how to connect student exploration and investigation of ideas to the development of scientific knowledge. Her Teacher Round opens up one episode of this fundamental process for inspection as part of a continuing discussion of practice within a small community of learners.

Phoebe's Teacher Round: Introduction to Constructive Critique in Art Class

Overview

It is mid-November and Phoebe is conducting her first Teacher Round as a teacher intern in the classroom of the 9th grade art class she has been teaching for several weeks at South High School. The classroom itself is a mosaic of past and current student artwork: pencil sketches, charcoal drawings, and more elaborate colored drawings compose a multicolored checkerboard on the walls. A group of rectangular tables, with black surfaces and stools alongside, forms a central square in the room. A table in their midst holds a collection of different objects of artistic interest, such as bottles and fruit. Above, mobiles dangle in an awkward but captivating array. It seems the kind of inviting space likely to coax into expression the artistic sensibilities of students who do not necessarily think of themselves as artists.

The students are in the midst of a study of contrast with Phoebe. As she describes it in her Round sheet, the study has entailed "examining how artists use opposing elements to create dramatic, eye-catching compositions." Along the way, the ninth graders worked on a still life project Phoebe called "Drawing like Da Vinci"—thus the odd assembly of bottles and fruits on the center table. They learned about "the elements of form (three dimensional objects) and value (the darkness or lightness of an object)" and the concepts of "local value" ("the overall value of an object without shadow or pattern") and "proportion" ("the size of an object relative to the other objects in a composition").

During the Round students will have an opportunity to apply their knowledge of contrast, local value, and proportion as Phoebe introduces them to the process of critique. Each student in a group of three will analyze samples of student work from another class—all resulting from the "Drawing like Da Vinci" activity—in terms of one of these three concepts. The groups of three will then discuss together their findings regarding each work.

The learning about form, contrast, and proportion is grounded in the time-honored process of peer critique in studio art. Still, there is a significant pedagogical challenge, as Phoebe considers what guidance and support her young apprentices need in order to perform the deceptively simple analytical tasks of seeing, assessing, and explaining what is in the drawings and to work together.

Round Partners

Rounds have become a customary practice in the small art wing of the school. Phoebe's mentor teacher is joined by the art teacher across the hall and another teacher intern who is teaching art, as well as a university mentor. Both the mentor teacher and his fellow art teacher participate on a team of visual art teachers with Phoebe's university mentor to discuss and develop their own practice. To some degree, Phoebe's Teacher Round reflects and extends the ongoing effort of the teachers to probe and stretch their own practice, to act as a discipline-based professional learning community.

Two other teacher interns—one who teaches mathematics, the other history—and another university mentor complete the group. Teacher interns who happen to be teaching in different disciplines stand to learn from the distinct disciplinary and pedagogical approaches they may see in a Teacher Round of one of their peers. The workshop and peer critique model that is highly developed in many arts classrooms, for example, may inform the effort to establish document analysis or writing groups in the classroom of the history teacher intern, or the problem-solving groups in the classroom of her mathematics counterpart.

Preround Orientation

Phoebe describes her unit on contrast and the progression of study from the elements of form of three dimensional objects and the concept of value (the darkness or lightness of an object) to the current focus of the class on understanding local value and proportion. She explains that novice artists "are timid in their artwork—they are reluctant to lay down a bold color or dark shadow." One of her unit goals is to encourage students to take the risks that will lead to the "courageous marks" and "bold, visual statements" characteristic of more advanced work. Phoebe's purpose today is to build students' understanding of how the concepts of contrast, local value, and proportion can be applied in drawings through the process of close examination and critique.

Phoebe sees critique both as an inherent part of artistic development and an integral part of the learning process. But the students are still at an early stage in developing their capacity to critique. They were reticent and uncertain during their first effort with Phoebe's mentor teacher. Phoebe's pedagogical challenge is how to build this capacity. Her baseline assumption is that students will develop their

Figure 3.4   Phoebe's Round Sheet

Background: The period 7 Art I students have just finished their pencil drawings of a still life from observation. This still life project, entitled "Drawing like Da Vinci," falls within our current unit on contrast, in which we have been examining how artists use opposing elements to create dynamic, eye-catching compositions. This project has furthered students' knowledge about the elements of form (three dimensional objects) and value (the darkness or lightness of an object). This project also introduced students to the concepts of local value (the overall value of an object without shadow or pattern) and proportion (the size of the object relative to other objects in a composition).

This is the first time I have done group work with this class, but I am confident in these students' ability to work together and also to listen to each other. I hope to take advantage of this class's social energy and channel it into this collaborative activity.

Learning focus: The primary focus of this learning activity is to familiarize students with the critique process in small groups so that they will feel more comfortable speaking up in the future during critiques involving the whole class. This activity will also teach students to analyze a piece of artwork by breaking it down into parts, in this case, contrast, local value, and proportion. I noticed that in our last critique involving the whole class, most students were reluctant to speak up and were unclear about what to say. This critique is structured with the aim of making students feel as comfortable as possible—they will be working in small groups to avoid the anxiety of public speaking, they will be critiquing the work of another class to avoid self-consciousness, and they will be given a specific lens through which to analyze the work, so that they will know the topic they need to address. For future critiques I will gradually remove some of these supports so that eventually students will feel comfortable analyzing work from their individual lens in front of the whole class.

Today students will be working in groups of three during an activity called the "critique carousel." In each group students will play three different roles—the contrast critiquer, the local value critiquer, or the proportion critiquer. I will give each group three still life drawings from a different Art I class to comment on through their particular lens. Once every critiquer has commented on all three works, I will ask the small groups to discuss their findings and to pick one still life to critique in front of the class, commenting on the drawing's contrast, local value, and proportion.

Round Inquiry

1. Participation: I have arranged the small groups so that there is a natural leader in each group. Within each group, is one student taking the lead or is everyone participating more or less equally. Are the English language learners getting support and participating?

2. Artistic literacy: Do students understand the concepts of contrast, local value, and proportion, or is there still some confusion?

3. My practice: What could I have done differently to make the instructions for the "critique carousel" more clear or run more smoothly?

4. The wrap-up: During the final portion of the lesson, when each group is critiquing one drawing in front of the whole class, are other students listening? Do students seem nervous or at ease while addressing the class as a whole?

capability and their willingness to exercise it when the concepts (contrast, local value, and proportion) are understandable, when they have practice seeing and assessing them in a work, and when they can present in a low-pressure environment. This idea leads to a four-part structure for the day: an opening review of the concepts; individual examination—based on one of the concepts—of three anonymous drawings taken from another beginner class (students will not be using their own drawings, Phoebe's effort to minimize self-consciousness) resulting in a short written analysis; sharing within groups of three, each student responsible for discussing each drawing in terms of the concept they were assigned to examine; and a wrap-up in which each group will present its findings to the whole class. She calls the individual and group process critique carousel. The critique carousel provides a high scaffold of support in Phoebe's view, one which she will lower over time, as she writes in her Round sheet: "For future critiques, I will gradually remove some of these supports so that eventually students will feel comfortable analyzing work from their individual lens in front of the whole class."

After clarifying her purpose and activity structure for the Round group, Phoebe outlines her strategy for organizing groups so as to harness natural leaders (students Phoebe judges will nurture others' involvement) to meet her additional pedagogical challenge—to encourage and more fully engage several English language learners (Round question #1). She also carefully explains the artistic concepts so that Teacher Round participants unfamiliar with them can look intelligently for evidence of student understanding during the Round (Round question #2).

The Round

Class begins when 10 girls and 10 boys gather and Phoebe draws their attention to the bell ringer, the simple opening task designed to stimulate individual thinking in relation to the day's work. Today, it consists of a slip of paper depicting a cartoonish art detective spouting artistic assessments—such as, "This drawing is too gray—boring!"—which students have to identify in terms of the concepts of contrast, local value, or proportion. This, Phoebe notes, is a refresher to prepare them for the process of group critique. She has projected the concepts onto a screen in the front of the room, and after reviewing the bell-ringer, asks for volunteers to explain each concept in turn. Different students offer "balance of black and white" to explain contrast and refer to "size of objects" in explaining proportion. Phoebe reminds them to focus on the "lights and darks" when looking at contrast and the overall value when looking at local value, not the shadow or detail. She seems satisfied that the students as a whole understand the concepts and are ready to assess them in the drawings she will give them. She emphasizes that the drawings are anonymous and that students in their written comments should explain *why* a drawing does or does not have the quality they are assigned to assess. The basis for their assessments—their thinking—is what matters.

As it turns out, not all students approach the task confident in what they are looking for. A girl in one group says to a peer that she is confused about local value, according to Phoebe the most difficult concept for students to grasp. Her partner is helpful, explaining that local value is "everything together as a whole" and suggests that "the background and shading could use more darkness." Phoebe encourages students to elaborate their thinking as she checks in on them. "Why do you think that?" she asks a student who says that "the bottle should stand out." The student adds to her critique sheet that the artist should "shade the bottle darker." Another student writes, "The drawing does not have enough contrast because the bottle does not have enough light shades to make it stand out and look more realistic as well as the banana." A partner determines that "they could also value the table a bit so the objects stand out more."

Groups huddle to share their individual assessments and to choose one of their two drawings to critique before the whole class. Phoebe wants them to develop their public voices as artists and the wrap-up will consist of their reports to the class and her comments on them. A single spokesperson represents some groups, while other groups distribute their reporting responsibility. The critiques have varying degrees of substance. Holding up their drawing, group #5 says that "it doesn't have balance between dark and white," "needs to add local value," and "the cylinder could be smaller." Pushing for more explanation, Phoebe asks for any other thoughts and the spokesperson for group #5 elaborates that the "cylinder could be a little lighter." Other groups are more explicit. One student maintains, "I think this artist has proportion because the soda can is drawn to scale." The group reports conclude the class.

Postround Reflection

Phoebe begins the postround conversation by noting the extent of student writing and the increase in interaction among students from previous classes. The structured individual writing and responsibility within the groups seems to have facilitated greater participation. The Teacher Round group focuses on the participation structure and student involvement, in keeping with Phoebe's first round question. Her mentor teacher notes that one English language learner was able to do the individual work but stood back from the group discussion. Another Round partner observes that another English learner, a native Spanish speaker, was helped by a group member. Phoebe identifies the helper as one of the natural leaders she assigned to the group and her mentor teacher adds that this is an example of group members complementing one another. Other observations suggest that the extent and nature of group member interaction varied from group to group. Two of the English language learners spoke during the wrap-up, a very encouraging sign for Phoebe, but others were not noticeably involved.

These observations, just as they are meant to do in a Teacher Round, serve as a springboard for reflection, in this case on the structure and content of the interaction. Phoebe relied on strategic group composition (for example, pairing an English learner with a natural leader) and the task of forming and sharing individual critiques to create interaction. But Round group members muse on possibilities for enhancing participation and the substance of discussion. One of Phoebe's peers suggests that structuring the critique in a more defined series of steps, using visuals, might have benefited everyone, in particular English learners. Another Round partner wonders whether a question forcing groups to take a stand on their assessments—for example, deciding which of their two drawings best represents the qualities of contrast, value, and proportion and why—would have stimulated more detailed and informative observations during the group discussion phase and wrap-up. Another adds that there may be value in stimulating a positive "subjective controversy" along these lines in terms of building the practice and culture of critique.

The other extensive thread of discussion stems from Phoebe's second Round question regarding student understanding of the concepts. One of Phoebe's fellow teacher interns thinks that most students know the terms. By way of example, she notes that she asked "What are you looking for?" and a student talked about the light and dark shades. There were many examples of students writing down partial or more developed observations of the drawings based on the concepts; many, however, were framed negatively, leaving Phoebe to ponder how to encourage critique as constructive and positive analysis. Phoebe's University mentor suggests that

Phoebe's structuring of the task to keep students' focus on the qualities of the drawings helped keep observations concrete; the alternative might have been more normative and less informative statements such as "This is good." At the same time, Phoebe's mentor teacher draws attention to the potential value of modeling or whole class critique after the bell ringer. These students, after all, are novices learning what to look for and how to assess and express it; Phoebe might have projected a single drawing, modeled the analytical thinking process by describing her own thoughts as she looked at the quality of contrast, and then guided students through additional close observation and assessment of the qualities of local value and proportion. Phoebe's mentor wonders further whether students might turn to their own work for a self-assessment, just as "real artists" do. This suggestion has immediate impact, as Phoebe's students do precisely that the next day.

Questions of Practice

The postround discussion was well grounded in observation that spoke directly to Phoebe's concerns for engaging all students, in particular English language learners, for developing public voices and for developing artistic literacy and a culture and capacity for critique. In this sense, it addressed well the particular curricular and social context of her class and provided perspective on the development of her students as artistic learners as well as the strength of her pedagogy—her adaptive expertise—in supporting them. All of the postround comments were thoughtfully present in the reflection on the Round she wrote afterwards.

More generally, the Round set in relief the question of how to induct a particular group of novice learners into the way of knowing of art—how to help them learn to see specific qualities of a drawing or their absence and understand their function and effectiveness, as well as how to engage in the individual and social process of critique. As suggested by her Round sheet, this particular lesson represented one in a likely series of adjustments Phoebe will make in developing her practice so that the students develop theirs. Phoebe, in essence, is learning to transform her classroom into a carefully structured and guided artists' workshop. Today she learned more about how to construct the curriculum and attend to her students' progress in learning in order to make that happen. Her Teacher Round checked and informed her pedagogy and practice at an early stage, adding to a continuing conversation she is having with her mentors and peers.

Jeremy S.'s Teacher Round: A Visual Introduction to the Great Depression

Overview

It is January and Jeremy, a teacher intern, has just begun a unit on the Great Depression with his 11th grade students. He has worked with these students since the beginning of the school year. Like all classes at UPCS, this one is untracked and heterogeneous. This is Jeremy's second Teacher Round.

Jeremy decides to exercise students' historical imaginations at this stage of the unit. Concerned that he may have been too text heavy in previous units, he will use audio and visual artifacts to introduce this one. During the previous day's class, students listened to "Brother, can you spare a dime?" and discussed the song's lament for the plight of workers left destitute in the country they have been instrumental in building. Today, they will enter into the experience of the Depression through photographs from the 1930s he has culled from online collections of the Library of Congress and National Archives. Jeremy's main goals are for students to learn to use photographs as primary sources and to develop an understanding of the wide and devastating impact of the Depression on the lives of people. He calculates that they will then be ready to study the era more deliberately.

Jeremy's underlying pedagogical question is how to help students use the photo images as historical artifacts to understand the impact of the Depression. His students are experienced working together to examine primary source texts; so Jeremy knows they understand issues such as author's point of view and historical context. But learning from the images will require a different kind of inspection—students must look for and interpret visual evidence and cues, whether intended or not, as to time, place, experience, and historical meaning.

There are several stages to the lesson: modeling, paired student work, paired student presentations, and a wrap-up to make a present-day connection. Jeremy will use a Depression-era photograph with the whole class to model the process of noticing what is in a visual image and imagining and narrating the experience of one of the people depicted. The students will then perform the same task in pairs, each pair using a different photograph. Each pair will display its photograph and narrate the imagined experience of one of the figures depicted in the photograph to the whole class. To help students connect past to present, Jeremy will conclude by showing a striking contemporary take on the photograph he uses as part of his initial engagement, based on the Hurricane Katrina disaster.

Round Partners

The Round group includes Jeremy's mentor teacher and university mentor, a history teacher visiting from another school, two of Jeremy's fellow history teacher interns, and two other teacher interns teaching in other disciplines.

Preround Orientation

During the preround conversation Jeremy explains his approach to introducing the students' study of the Depression through personal experience as reflected in music and photographic images. He mentions that the work of today will contribute to a broader scrapbook project on the period that students will develop and which will help him assess their historical understanding.

The visiting history teacher directs attention to Jeremy's central pedagogical question, asking whether there are "any steps?" in how Jeremy will ask the students to look at the photograph. Jeremy responds that he will ask students to address four things: what the figures in the photograph are doing and when, how they are feeling, and what might be next in their experience. Here Jeremy focuses on "the what" more than "the how"—on what he hopes students will determine rather than how they might go about determining it. He does explain that he will ask students "what they notice" in the photograph that they will look at together to start the class—noticing is an accessible starting point for seeing and interpreting. Jeremy is thinking about his discipline-specific pedagogy, specifically how to translate historical norms for analyzing primary source texts to the study of images. But, as the Round will reveal, there is more that he can do on the way to making this a solid practice for him and his students.

The Round

Jeremy projects "At the Time of the Louisville Flood," a 1937 photograph by Margaret Bourke-White. What appears to be a billboard looms in the background with the headline, "World's Highest Standard of Living," followed by "There's no way like the American Way." The billboard is completed by the image of a smiling white

Figure 3.5   Jeremy's Round Sheet

Background: The students in this untracked classroom have just begun a unit on the Great Depression. Their final project for this unit is a diary/scrapbook assignment due at the end of next week. This project will allow students to interpret a variety of sources through different perspectives. For example, they listened to the song, "Brother, can you spare a dime?" (1931) and compared it to Wyclef Jean's recession hit, "Sweetest Girl" from 2007, with which most were already familiar. Additionally, they watched the film Seabiscuit (2003) based on Laura Hillenbrand's book and have a general idea of what happened during the Great Depression.

Learning Focus: This learning activity focuses on photo-analysis skills and the ability to see what is happening in a photograph from a different perspective. It also will engage students' historical imaginations, as they will use photographic images as a basis for imagining the experience and impact of the Great Depression, building on their study over a number of classes.

Low-stakes journal writing will introduce basic analysis before students work as pairs to write their own brief first person narrative of what they think the people in the image are experiencing. We will discuss the first image as a class. I will provide scaffolding if students do not notice the text behind the line of people in the photograph waiting for food. Photos show a variety of issues that could be more deeply researched for their scrapbook projects.

Once pairs are made, students will write a paragraph-long first person narrative on their photo sheet. They have 10 minutes to complete this step. Afterward, pairs will display their image on the document reader and tell their story to the class. Students in the audience will therefore be exposed to more images, which will inform their scrapbook projects. During the presentations, students should take notes on any points that will strengthen their projects.

Round Inquiry

1. Document investigation skills: Are students taking time to notice what is in their image before writing about it?

2. Historical thinking: Are students questioning the photographs and hypothesizing what they are seeing in terms of what they know about the period of the Great Depression (historical context)?

3. Participation: Are they writing collaboratively, or is one partner dominating the process?

4. Curriculum goals: Do you notice students thinking about their scrapbook project as they analyze photos or watch presentations?

family in a car, dog panting out the window. In stark contrast to the billboard image, unsmiling people of color are queued up in the foreground with empty baskets and bags in hand, what appears to be a small white boy standing near the line's end.

In response to Jeremy's writing prompt, all students write what they notice in the photograph. Jeremy selects several volunteers to offer an example to the whole class. One student refers to "the highest standard of living" phrase and people standing in line. A second suggests ironically that "they seem to be living less than the highest standard." Jeremy shows good wait time as this student formulates his next thought: "So it's like a satire basically." A third student notices that "the line is mostly African-American" and wonders whether that reflects segregation and "racism going on" at the time; no one, however, points out the contrast between the people of color in the line and the smiling white family in the hovering image of the car. Jeremy, in response, reminds students of the theme of racial division that emerged in the previous day's discussion; this connection does not evoke further probing by students or more prompting by Jeremy; but the theme emerges again before the end of class. Modeling what he is asking students to do, Jeremy proceeds to read a sample narrative from the perspective of one of the people standing in line.

Students quickly transition to working in pairs with the photographs Jeremy has given to each pair. Many of the photographs are arresting and draw students' attention. One pair examines Dorothea Lange's "Migrant Mother" (1936); yet so taken are they by the image of the mother that they neglect to consider details related to the two young boys, heads turned away and bowed to hers, who frame her careworn face. Other pairs also focus more on foregrounded and central images in their photographs, just as the class as a whole did in examining "At the Time of the Louisville Flood."

After examining a photograph, each pair decides on a figure to whom to give a historical voice and writes from that perspective. The writing takes place in different ways; in most cases, students talk about what to write, with one student taking initial responsibility. In some cases, one partner writes and hands over the script for review and expansion by the other. Jeremy and other Round participants circulate to the pairs, asking students what they see, who they will write about, and what they surmise is the experience of that figure and why.

Student pairs present findings from their inspections of the photographs and read their narrations in fairly rapid order, Jeremy trying to give every pair the opportunity before class ends. One student notes the segregated facilities and, adopting a postracial society stance, says that they were "still racist back then." Jeremy confirms that "racial segregation was alive and well at this time." There is little opportunity for questioning and feedback. Time slips away and Jeremy's planned wrap-up—using a contemporary political cartoon which evokes the photograph he displayed to begin the lesson—will have to wait until the next day's class.

Postround Reflection

The postround discussion focuses on several themes, based principally on Jeremy's first three Round questions:

Noticing detail and using images for historical study

One thread of discussion focuses on the extent to which students noticed detail in the photograph Jeremy uses as part of his initial engagement with the whole class and in the photographs they examine in pairs. Many students attend to some details and not others or to the most prominent details at the expense of smaller but no less telling ones (e.g., in Lange's photograph of the "Migrant Mother" and her children or in the photographs showing evidence of racially segregated facilities). One Round partner suggests drawing a tighter parallel with the class's previous work with written primary sources. Students learn to look for clues about the author and the historical context—to think historically—with written source material. What if students had more practice doing the same with visual images? Many, in haste to get to their assignment to write a short narrative, otherwise neglect detail valuable for developing deeper appreciation and a more fine-grained analysis. To slow down the process and cultivate the skill of noticing, what if Jeremy dedicated a specific amount of time, perhaps 2 minutes, to examining the photographs before giving the writing assignment? In a related suggestion, one member of the Round group wonders whether students might spend time looking at several photographs in their pairs rather than looking only at one—more direct engagement with several photographs may be more beneficial than listening to all-too-short analyses by other pairs.

Historical questioning

Round participants also focus briefly on the question of linking the photographs more concretely to the historical context and content. Is there an opportunity for students to generate historical questions from looking at the photographs? Students use their historical imaginations to construct a probable narrative of experience, but what more can they learn about the history, the historical context? Student questions about segregation, for example, might lead to a mini-investigation on the effect of the Depression on African Americans living in different regions of the country, particularly in places where issues of poverty and race converged. The idea of treating history as inquiry might be built more directly into the pairs work—"what questions do the images raise for you about the historical period of the Depression?"

The postround conversation pays an immediate dividend: Jeremy says he will apply some of the ideas discussed in a class later in the day. And he does. He allows for more depth by modeling and extending the time for students to notice detail before moving to interpretation and writing. Students looked at fewer photographs more carefully. As Jeremy wrote afterward, "I decided each student did not need exposure to each photo to capture the essence of the lesson and to see the destitution of the Great Depression. Rather than passively see all 12 photos through the eyes of their peers, they individually analyzed about half of them." He also adjusts the timing of each part of the lesson, leaving room for investigation of the political cartoon based on Hurricane Katrina—with which students are familiar—which echoes the 1937 image from the Depression. Finally, he reconsidered the benefit of having students share out, instead reallocating the sharing time for individual writing. As he reported, "My round taught me to develop a keener sense of tempo in the classroom. . . . Also, it led me to consider the value of sharing out. . . . I ensured accountability in the second period by collecting their work. Otherwise, a more organic and productive discussion developed, unlike the observed class period, in which I frantically pushed groups along without leaving time for student discussion and questioning" (J. Sanders, personal communication, January 27, 2012).

Questions of Practice: Developing a Discipline-Specific Pedagogy

Jeremy's Teacher Round raises questions about historical investigation using visual images, about how to engage students in uncovering, substantiating, or questioning the visual and historical content. It suggests the value of giving students time and practice in noticing detail and modeling this investigative process, of student-generated questions based on the detail, of relating visual to text-based sources, and of demonstrating the iconic power of photographs not only to connect the historical with everyday human experience with which students can empathize but also to show the relevance of the past and present to each other (which Jeremy taps in comparing images related to the 1937 Louisville flood and Katrina). These suggestions are building blocks not only for Jeremy's pedagogical repertoire but for the practice of his peers who attended his Round. And they magnify more generally the dynamic and adaptive nature of teaching expertise—teaching as a series of adjustments in relation to curricular and disciplinary goals based on attention to different students and their interaction with subject matter. That they were developed in concert, as Jeremy's written reflection suggests, also indicates the value of classroom-based, collaborative learning for these developing teachers.

Jeremy's Preround Orientation: Immersion in the *Odyssey*

Standing in the corridor outside his classroom at UPCS, Jeremy, an English teacher intern on his way to becoming a full-time teacher at the school, describes his plan to lead his 9th grade students on a foray into Homer's *Odyssey*. Recognizing the foreignness of the language, form, and genre for his students, Jeremy explains that he has paved the way carefully, appropriating clips from the movie *Troy* (with which most students are familiar), a passage from *The Illiad*, and an essay on "Homer and the Epic." He has also read with students the picture book *Where the Wild Things Are*, accessible to all and familiar to many, "to scaffold the word *odyssey* and discuss the meaning of returning home."

Today Jeremy will concentrate on the "invocation" of the *Odyssey*, Homer's opening declaration of the heroic story he will tell, seeking "help and inspiration" from the goddess Muse. Students will revise the invocation formula that they constructed in the previous class after dissecting, working in pairs, the characteristics of the invocation. In their formula, students took note of Homer's emphasis, in terms of content, on hero, struggle, and obeisance to the gods; and, in terms of form, the fact that the invocation is narrated in the third person and that it is told directly to the Muse. In constructing the invocation formula, students have prepared the basis for assessing their future work: the invocation formula will serve as the rubric by which their own invocations will be judged.

Jeremy's main learning goal for the day is to solidify students' understanding of the characteristics of Homer's invocation, inching them more deeply into Homer's world. One of his strategies for reaching this goal is to have students critique his own invocation. In his rendition, he will highlight his role as teacher and his hopes for his students; students will then decide whether he has been faithful to the Odyssey's form and characteristics. Students will demonstrate their understanding further by writing an invocation about themselves. Jeremy wants to immerse students in the epic form and framework so that it is familiar and accessible and holds meaning for them. His effort to connect disciplinary learning, content, and pedagogy distinguish the remainder of the preround discussion. Jeremy's university mentor asks questions that help clarify Jeremy's assessment of his students' understanding of the epic genre and invocation and also the structural and conceptual framework students will use to write their own invocations, following Jeremy's model. One of Jeremy's Round questions reflects his pedagogical aim to foster his students' understanding of both genre and content: "During the think-pair-share, do students make active use of what they have learned about invocations, vocabulary, and knowledge of the epic tradition to accurately evaluate my invocation model?"

Later, after his Teacher Round had occurred, Jeremy reported that he had "students memorize their invocations, since epic poets during Homer's time were not merely reading their narratives but *reciting* them. Each class . . . began with a student going to the front of the room to recite their invocation. This was especially cool, because at the start of every class, before we dove back into the pages of *The Odyssey*, a different student was invoking the Muse, almost asking for assistance as we embarked on the epic task of reading this challenging text" (J. Murphy, personal communication, June 15, 2012). As Jeremy had hoped, students continued to immerse themselves in the text and its form.

4

Sharing and Developing Expertise in Elementary School

The Teacher Round protocol can be applied equally well regardless of grade or school level or curriculum. This chapter illustrates Teacher Round learning at the elementary level. It begins with a detailed presentation of a Teacher Round focused on early guided reading in a 2nd grade classroom. The remainder of the chapter centers on the experience of two teachers and exemplifies one way in which a school can use Teacher Rounds to anchor its effort to build and sustain effective practice. These examples demonstrate the learning that is possible, for both teachers and students, when there is a safe space, openness, and courage to learn.

Margaret's Teacher Round: Early Guided Reading (Grade 2)

Overview

Margaret is the literacy coach for Woodland Academy, a K–6 school. Her Teacher Round occurs in a 2nd grade classroom. It is

September and students are still adjusting to the school year, many also to a return to daily reading. The majority of students in the school are nonnative English speakers. Almost all qualify for the federal free or reduced lunch program.

Margaret works with six students, four boys and two girls, at a crescent moon-shaped desk. The students are developing readers at an early stage, spanning the D-I levels on the scale used by Fountas and Pinnell. Margaret has some information about the students' needs as young readers but little about their interests and personalities. As she points out in her Round sheet, she feels her lack of knowledge will limit the extent to which she can be "authentic" in the lesson: the students "are complex individuals. They are not just their reading level!" She would rather draw on a greater understanding of what these students think, feel, and need in her effort to support their development as readers. Nevertheless, she is intent on supporting them in the lesson and in implementing the guided reading process.

Guided reading places explicit emphasis on a teacher's ability to frame, attend to, and scaffold a student's effort to learn. Margaret's lesson sets this process in high relief for the Round group: participants will have an opportunity to observe closely how and how well different students go about comprehending and thinking about the text and how Margaret goes about understanding and supporting students' meaning-making and development as readers.

Margaret introduces students to a new nonfiction book, *The Fantastic Flying Squirrel.* The book is at the I reading level. It should be accessible to all students but will be more challenging for some than others.

Round Partners

The Round group is a mix of several teachers and instructional aides at the school, including the new 2nd grade classroom teacher and an English as Second Language (ESL) teacher, and several teacher interns. The teacher interns are accompanied by their university mentor.

Preround Orientation

Margaret reviews the early guided reading lesson plan that she prepared. She points out the prompts for early readers that she will use, which she has listed on the plan, to help students as needed in their effort to comprehend the text:

Figure 4.1 Margaret's Round Sheet

Background: This lesson focuses on early guided reading, as these students are in the D-I reading range. Please bear in mind that this experience can never be as authentic as I would like! I am not the classroom teacher and so don't know these students as readers, although I have some information from their teacher. But, of course, in order to plan an effective lesson, you need to know each student really well: what do they love? What are they scared of? What do they find easy or difficult, and so on? They are complex individuals. They are not just their reading level!

Learning Focus: I will introduce a new book, *The Fantastic Flying Squirrel*, which is about animals that sleep during the day and stay awake at night. We will concentrate on comprehending the text and corresponding photographs. The students should be able to identify important ideas in the text and report them in an organized way. During the individual reading phase, I will pay particular attention to moments in which students seem unsure or uncomprehending and will try to understand how they are making sense of the text, using various prompts, such as "What makes sense? What are you thinking about? How can you help yourself?" I expect to support different students in different ways in their reading by helping them to think about and utilize word-solving strategies.

Through the Round process, I would like to learn as much as possible about how different students go about reading and understanding the book and whether and how my efforts help their understanding and their continued development as readers. Therefore, for the Round inquiry, I suggest that you take notes on what I do and what students do and record your reflections and questions. I have suggested a three-column note taker for this purpose.

Round Inquiry

What I saw/heard the teacher say/do	What I saw/heard the students say/do	Questions

- Check the picture and think what would make sense.
- Does it look right and make sense?
- Reread the sentence.
- Cover the ending. Is there a part you know?
- Do you know another word that looks like this one?
- What can you do to help yourself?

If she judges that students all have a basic understanding of the book, then she will ask them to write one sentence about what the book is about—to articulate their sense of the book's main purpose or idea.

Margaret explains her interest in having the Round group record what she and the students say and do—to generate a record of the guided reading process that they can discuss during the postround reflection. Primed for their role as observers, members of the Round group take seats somewhat behind and to the right of Margaret.

The Round

The guided reading session unfolds in four basic stages: prereading, individual guided reading (the longest stage), individual writing, and group sharing and discussion.

During the prereading stage, which lasts about 5 to 7 minutes, Margaret draws attention to different photos and words in the text, asking questions about them, gauging students' prior knowledge, and also preparing them for the subject and language of the book. She points out that the author is in the "woods" but doesn't use the word. She asks if students see a similar word that the author uses; "forest" is one reply. In another instance, she says the author "uses a special word" instead of "flies" to describe the flight of the squirrels—"when they don't flap wings"—and draws the students' attention to the word, *glides*. She then suggests that students read the whole book individually and think about the most important part—"if you were to tell a first grader." She softly instructs students to use their voices if they wish, but be "very quiet." Students proceed to look at the photographs in the book and to read, most aloud, producing a blend of low and whispered tones.

Margaret turns her attention to individual students as they read, taking notes. In her own low voice, she matter-of-factly responds to moments of uncertainty with one or more of her planned prompts—"What makes sense? What else can you do to help yourself? What are you thinking?" In one instance, referring to the strategy of rereading to see what makes sense, she says, "Check and see if you're right . . . OK, keep going!"

One particular boy—Student A—draws most of Margaret's attention. He hesitates in his reading at the word *asleep* in the sentence which begins, "Many animals are asleep." After asking what he is thinking, Margaret learns that he wants the word to be *sleeping*. She responds, affirming his attention to meaning, that "*sleeping* makes sense, but something's not quite right: What sound do you hear at the beginning of *sleeping*?" When Student A makes a sibilant "s" sound, Margaret redirects his attention to "the tricky word." Student A says, "Oh, it's *asleep*!" Margaret asks, "How do you know?" and Student A points out the "a" sound at the beginning of the word. Margaret asks him to try rereading the first part of the sentence "now that you've fixed the tricky part," and he does so accurately. The second part of the sentence reads, "but some are waking up." He substitutes *awake* for *waking up*. But this time Margaret does not intervene.

In the final part of the lesson, when all students have completed the reading, Margaret returns to the question she posed at the outset: what would they tell a first grader is the most important part of the book? Determining what is important momentarily becomes a group endeavor, with Margaret asking students what they can add to one student's idea. Students also work on writing one sentence about what is important; one or two have difficulty starting, and Margaret asks them to tell her what they are thinking about in an effort to help them discover what they might say. Students also share their ideas with those sitting beside them.

During whole group sharing, a new question enters the conversation: whether the book is fiction or nonfiction and what in the book would help you to know. There is a long pause, while Margaret waits patiently for student thought to form. Some students are uncertain; both genres otherwise have advocates. A girl who sides with nonfiction offers "pictures" as a reason. "Tell me more about pictures," Margaret responds. The girl mentions, "camera," and Margaret asks for "hands up" if students agree that the author used a camera. This is accepted as a reason for the book being nonfiction, without time for elaborating why.

In the final moments, Margaret asks, "What do you think you learned today that will help you as a reader tomorrow?" Student A, who pondered *asleep* and *awake*, says, "[It's] good to read two times." One of his peers boldly amplifies the idea: "[It's] good to read three times."

Postround Reflection

Margaret begins the postround by reviewing briefly the beginning part of the lesson, when she introduced the book. Then, prompted by observations and questions from members of the Round group, she talks in detail about Student A's individual reading, explaining why she responded in the way that she did at two important moments in her interaction with him. The postround ends with a short reflection on the sentences the students wrote to explain the idea of the book and what they suggest about the students' comprehension. Overall, Margaret's interaction with Student A becomes a focal point and assumes broader significance as a lens for thinking about teacher purpose and practice—and adaptive expertise—in the guided reading process.

In reflecting on her introduction of the book, Margaret notes her overriding concern for keeping students attuned to the meaning of what they would be reading. It was important for instance, especially for the English learners, to connect prior knowledge of the word *woods* to the less familiar word, *forest*, without distracting them by introducing in addition the concept of synonym.

Attention turns to Margaret's interaction with Student A. When Student A hesitated at a word he was unsure about, Margaret noticed that he looked up. Margaret interpreted this as a reflexive action, as an expectation that she would provide an answer for him—"he's learned that if he looks up, [then he will be] told the word." For that reason, she sat so as "not to make eye contact" with him when he became puzzled; "If he goes back, he can figure out words." When he understands a word, she asks him if he is right rather than offer a perfunctory "good job!" It is important, she says, to "leave them with some work to do." She is trying to help Student A gain confidence in his own word-deciphering ability, to internalize the strategies that will help him help himself.

When Student A pauses at the word *asleep* while reading aloud, Margaret uses a series of prompts both to understand what he is thinking and to build his own word-solving prowess. Learning that Student A wanted to read *asleep* as *sleeping* was revealing. One member of the Round group suggests that Student A is thinking about familiar patterns of spoken language. Margaret agrees: "He's predicting from [what he knows]. He's in transition between speech and print." Margaret's emphasis on reading for meaning explains her decision not to intervene when Student A substitutes *waking up* for *awake*. Margaret explains her judgment that another interruption in the flow of meaning might be one too many—"It wasn't interfering with his meaning so I let it go."

The postround reflection concludes with Margaret reading the sentences students wrote to convey their sense of the main idea of the book. The sentences tell specific facts rather than provide a general view. Examples are: "The flying squirrel jumps high." "Flying squirrels are very hungry." The Round group wonders how to account for the focus on facts rather than something broader. One idea is that students simply wrote a fact which attracted their interest rather than thinking about the book as a whole. Margaret notes that she did not model what the main idea of a book might be, implying that she assumed students would know. This suggests a point of departure should Margaret or the classroom teacher revisit the question of the main idea of the book with these young readers again.

The combination of observations and questions by members of the Round group and Margaret's explanation of what she did and why made teaching practice and student learning transparent to a degree that allowed for reflective understanding of this early guided reading lesson. The postround discussion highlighted the challenge of balancing the goal of comprehension with the need to give students comprehension tools such as word recognition and word-solving strategies. In more general terms, Margaret and members of the Round group were engaged in understanding the dynamic of purpose, assessment, and response particular to guided reading. They delved into the expertise entailed—the respect for each child's effort, the close listening and careful prompting in order to understand each child's way of apprehending and making sense of the text, and each child's progress as a reader, the ways of responding so as to help each child understand and learn on his or her own, the art of helping each student share and check his or her understandings and how he or she arrived at them—and how to apply it in their linguistically diverse context. They were reminded also of how such expertise respects the contingency of teaching: Margaret did not do all that she planned, but she suggested, in so many words, that in teaching which hews closely to what children are thinking, doing, and feeling, less can indeed be more.

Teacher Rounds at Jacob Hiatt Elementary School

Teacher Rounds have been valued by teachers at the Jacob Hiatt Elementary School for many years as a means to share and develop their practice in support of a largely low income and ethnically and linguistically diverse student body. In a typical year, teachers participate in two or three Round cycles. For them a cycle is a set of three or four Teacher Rounds spread out over a week or so. Every teacher participates, with as many as 10 teachers attending a given Round. Coverage provided by specialist teachers, administrators, or several substitute teachers hired for the purpose affords the time necessary to sandwich the preround orientation and postround reflection tightly around the Round.

The Teacher Round cycles are initiated by teachers or administrators, usually during a focused discussion on practice either in the school's instructional leadership team, during common planning time, or at an all-school staff meeting. The Round teacher is always a volunteer; well more than half of the teachers at the school have assumed the role. Individual teachers are sometimes coaxed by teachers or administrators to take the lead, especially if a teacher has a known strength in practice from which others want to learn. Once a Round cycle is set up, an e-mail notification alerts the entire staff to the schedule, and a sign-up sheet in the staff room serves as a means to organize the Round groups, unless a particular grouping based on a common interest has been determined at the outset. The Teacher Rounds usually represent a significant grade span—for example, grades 1, 3, 5 or 2, 4, 6. Typically, the teachers attending a given Teacher Round come from different grade levels; the teachers have developed a keen sense of how to apply what they learn in and from practice at one grade level to another. In fact, as Jen, a veteran 2nd grade teacher, explains, teachers strive to build "continuity" and "streamline" their "best practice" language across grade levels.

Self-Determined Teacher Rounds

At the school, the focus of a Teacher Round is either a matter of individual choice or common interest. In one cycle, individual teachers might focus the Round learning on their own very particular questions about teaching-learning in their classrooms. As Jen puts it, teachers are motivated by the question, "Are we being successful in what we are trying to achieve [in our classrooms]?" (J. Conlon, personal communication, June 5, 2012). Self-determined Teacher Rounds provide teachers with an opportunity to get feedback on an area of practice on which they are working. They contribute to a learning culture in which teachers respect each other's individual questions and personal trajectories of development.

The opportunity for collaborative learning can be unexpected. Sue, a veteran 3rd grade teacher, recalls a Teacher Round during which she was conducting an author study (S. Allen, personal communication, June 5, 2012). When the students' thoughts took an entirely unforeseen turn, she was momentarily at a loss, literally saying to her colleagues, "I'm looking for help now." Recovering her presence of mind, Sue says, "I had to go with kids' ideas." In this moment, adjusting to the flow of the kids' thinking, rather than trying to reroute them, proved productive. Discussion of how she adapted, and what it meant in terms of her learning goals, became the dominant theme of postround reflection. Jen remembers a similar experience. In her case, she was thrown off balance by the students' puzzling response to the central text-based question of her Round lesson. The students' ideas were far removed from the text they were considering. She finally recognized that the question simply had too many moving parts; her second graders gravitated, as we all might, to what made the most sense to them. She, too, had to respond and modify in the moment, rephrasing her question and redirecting students.

For both teachers, the Round experience pivoted on the unexpected and fateful turns a lesson can take. Both were challenged to assess the course of learning in the moment and decide how to respond. For both, the Round became an opportunity to reflect on the dynamics of teaching-learning: to revisit the structure of a lesson, to consider attentively what students are doing and saying and why, and to adapt according to one's best judgment of what will be valuable for students' learning. Both teachers valued the collaboration of peers in the process; they were building adaptive expertise together.

"Exemplary" and Theme-Based Teacher Rounds

In many Teacher Round cycles at Jacob Hiatt Elementary School, teachers address a common theme, chosen because of concern for student performance or a desire to learn about exemplary practice in a high-priority area. The Round Teachers are recognized as exemplary, are at the leading edge of practice in the area relative to others, or otherwise are willing to try. In their last Teacher Round cycle, teachers focused on how to engage students in reading nonfiction texts. The Teacher Rounds raised questions about general and discipline-specific features of nonfiction texts, in particular texts in science and social studies; about how nonfiction texts enter the English Language Arts curriculum; and about how to help students distinguish the features of nonfiction texts and learn from them.

Jen was one of the Round Teachers during the cycle on reading nonfiction texts. She focused her Round on how well her second graders, very much novices in the genre, "recognize and understand features of a nonfiction text." On her Round sheet, Jen explains that her children will read an article about the Youth Winter Olympic Games. Students "will be asked to mark nonfiction text features with a sticky note" and "share their findings." With Jen's guidance, the class will compile nonfiction text features on a single chart. Students then "will use turn and talk to define text features they have learned to each other." They will conclude with a shared reading of the text. Jen has a twofold Round inquiry. She wants Round participants to pay close attention to what students are doing and saying—with their sticky notes, in whole class discussion, and within their pairs—in order to determine whether and how they understand nonfiction texts and, by extension, the effectiveness of her instructional strategies. She also solicits examples of what she does or says to elicit and clarify student ideas. As in all Teacher Rounds at the school, participants are reminded to "record facts and evidence" on the Round sheet and that the process is nonevaluative. The teachers conclude the postround reflection by offering two things that they learn, two that they wonder about, and one significant takeaway. The learning, however, by no means ends with the postround. "Exemplary" Teacher Rounds such as Jen's are often videotaped for later use by individuals or by a larger group at a faculty meeting. In this way, they help build communal understanding of practice compatible with the school's learning goals.

"Opening Yourself (and Students) Up"

For Jen, the postround reflections are the most valuable part of the Teacher Round process, a chance to discuss practice in context— taking into account what you did "to prepare kids and where you are going." Both Jen and Sue talk about the value of their Teacher Rounds in terms of helping them understand if they are "on the right track" in their teaching; in Sue's words, they "help you evolve as a stronger teacher."

Jen reflects on the "process of opening yourself up" in Teacher Rounds: "You think [hard] about the questions you are going to ask and what response they will elicit. It's very reflective." Sue adds that "Once you've delved that deeply into things," your questions get reflected in the lesson. And you learn that "the children automatically go into depth" also. Jen considers her Teacher Round on reading nonfiction texts an example of this dynamic parallel between teacher and student learning at work. The reflective acts of planning the Teacher Round and discussing with peers where she would go next resulted in her being "even more explicit" in her teaching about the features of nonfiction texts. In following classes she "often referred back to what we had done in the lesson to be sure that children indeed retained what they had learned and had integrated it into their toolboxes for reading and understanding nonfiction texts. Later, [the Teacher Round lesson] also was integral to my teaching of writing nonfiction texts. Many children used the features that they had learned about when writing nonfiction animal research books." For Jen and her students, the Teacher Round sharpened the focus of their learning, encouraging "a deeper level of engagement."

Developing Expertise

Both Jen and her students were involved in studying, analyzing, and practicing. For Jen, the process of explaining and sharing her practice led to a closer examination of it, and heightened her own awareness and attentive effort. Her young students, meanwhile, were engaged in their own practice, going about the serious academic work of applying their knowledge of the characteristics of nonfiction texts to their writing. Both students and their teacher were developing expertise, both through a process of learning within community.

5

Rounds Day at University Park Campus School

University Park Campus School (UPCS) exemplifies how a school can integrate Teacher Rounds into its professional culture in order to develop a coherent practice in support of student learning. Teacher Rounds are second nature to the teachers and a familiar part of the landscape of learning for students as well. A typical "Rounds Day" at UPCS demonstrates the learning potential of Teacher Rounds as the practice takes root in a school.

Rounds Day

Today is "Rounds Day" at UPCS. Every teacher will host a Teacher Round and participate in at least two others. Every teacher and professional staff member will attend them. The school is small, with 16 full-time teachers in core subject areas (English, history, mathematics, physical and natural sciences) serving 250 students spanning grades 7 through 12. Teachers and staff will combine with teacher interns assigned to the school to provide coverage of classes as necessary to enable all teachers to participate. The Teacher Rounds will take place all day long.

Introduction to University Park Campus School

UPCS is a public school in an urban setting; by most educational measures, it is an extraordinary one (The Education Trust, November 1, 2005; U.S. Department of Education, August 15, 2005). There is no tracking but rather heterogeneous grouping combined with extended and supplemental learning periods. Instruction starts from a belief in every student as a thinker and a capable learner and from a commitment to help students realize their capability. Teachers work to personalize support for students and to help them learn to learn together. After four years at the school, most 10th grade students are at a "proficient" or "advanced" level in English and mathematics according to results on the statewide standardized test. Every student qualifies for some level of postsecondary education upon graduation. At least 75 percent persist in completing a four-year degree within six years. A handful of students every year take advantage of the promise by the school's university partner to provide admitted students with a tuition-free undergraduate education.

Yet, so much about UPCS belies its record of success. The cramped school facility, built to house neighborhood elementary-age children in the late 19th century, carries its faded Victorian-era architecture wearily; the elementary school across the street and the university two blocks away make up for the lack of a library and gymnasium. Nearby, unkempt three-story houses betray the struggle of the neighborhood and its people—so many of whom are caught up in a flux of movement in and out of rented spaces and the schools—to find a foothold for their lives over and against deterioration and uncertainty. Where dilapidated houses dominate, however, there are also new ethnic food stores, energetic church-based groups, and a neighborhood garden. A new Boys and Girls Club and bright new low-income housing reclaim land as well as neighborhood dignity about a half dozen blocks away, thanks to partnering between the local community development corporation, the university, and others. The demographic profile of UPCS students reflects the challenges of the neighborhood as well as its cultural richness: most students are considered low income based on the federal free or reduced lunch standard and two-thirds speak a language other than English at home.

Conceived as a joint venture of the university and the local school district in the mid-1990s, with the aim of creating an educational oasis in the neighborhood and preparing all students for college, UPCS thrives in the face of long odds. The Rounds day, a deliberate deep dive into culture and practice at the school, provides a glimpse of why.

Teacher Rounds at UPCS

Rounds are woven into the fabric of professional life at UPCS. Teachers host them to share their practice with teacher interns from their university partner and to introduce their practice to the many visitors drawn to the school because of its impressive performance record. Teacher interns at the school each conduct three Rounds over the course of the year, accounting for 18 or 21 of the dozens occurring there annually.

To understand why Teacher Rounds are a frequent form of dialogue and reflection on practice at UPCS, one must also understand the central values that anchor the learning culture for the principal, teachers, and students at the school. Teacher Rounds are emblematic of a strong student-centered, learning-centered, and collaborative culture and practice. Teachers regularly share and build their practice together through activities such as Teacher Rounds for the simple reason that they can attend that much more closely to students and their learning and what supports them along the path to becoming sound thinkers, readers, and writers— along the path to becoming responsible and college-ready learners. And they can do that together with genuine assurance that they will be supported: the process is viewed as educative—a matter of mutual learning—not evaluative. For Dan, who was introduced to Teacher Rounds when he was a teacher intern at the school, the intimate process of learning in each other's classrooms, as strange as it might be in some professional cultures, is customary, "Since we were trained that way. . . . [It is] so ingrained in us, how we think about ourselves. Interest in what each other is doing and what kids are doing is our default." Bob, the instructional coach, emphasizes that Rounds at the school are powerful because they foster "authentic adult learning" and a common learning culture. Ricci, principal and teacher of one class, adds that the fact of teachers collaborating "rubs off" on the kids, it is "just who we are . . . authentic deep thinking and inquiry" help form the learning culture—and sense of mutuality—for adults and students, one mirroring the other.

The Rounds Day Focus

Rounds Day at UPCS is a special opportunity for the teachers, as well as support staff, to compare notes on their actual practice and students' learning. Today, instead of organizing Rounds by grade level or discipline, they plan for more cross-cutting conversation.

They are especially interested in how colleagues in different disciplines and at different grade levels implement the school's shared instructional framework. The common framework stresses modes of active learning calculated to foster student capability and confidence as readers, writers, speakers, thinkers, and collaborators:

- Writing is used throughout the curriculum as a thinking tool.
- Talk and collaboration—focused on texts, problems, and questions—are cultivated so as to foster the exchange and careful development of ideas.
- Questioning, by students as well as teachers, emphasizes that inquiry is at the heart of learning.
- Teachers use various forms of scaffolding to engage students and develop their content understanding.

As a result of the Rounds day, teachers, principal, and staff members expect to learn more about how they are cultivating all students' academic capabilities and about the trajectory of students' learning toward college readiness. They expect to learn more about the progress and habits of learning of particular students. They also expect to learn more about practices which fulfill their instructional framework. Finally, they expect to generate some questions or issues on which they might collectively, or in groups, devote more attention. The timing is good—it is December, close to the midpoint of the year. Another Rounds day is planned for spring.

Rounds Day Organization

The Rounds day is organized by Bob, the instructional coach. Bob produces a schedule that allows preround conversations and actual Rounds to occur on a single day. These will be followed the next morning by postround conversations, during the normally scheduled weekly faculty meeting. Weekly faculty meetings are held during the first hour or so of school each Wednesday while specialty classes are offered for younger students and older students participate in morning community service or internships.

Here's what the schedule looks like:

Day 1

7:30–8:00 Preround discussions

8:00–2:23 Teacher Rounds (most classes are one hour long; one class is longer by 23 minutes)

Day 2

8:00–9:00 Postround discussions (individual Round groups)

9:00–9:30 Discipline-based groups discuss what they have learned

Schoolwide observations and discussion

Preround Discussions

Teachers and staff gather casually in Kevin's middle school English room, coffee in hand, before the 7:30 a.m. start of the preround conversations. All of the teachers will do their prerounds at the beginning of the day, regardless of when they will actually teach. Bob has several clusters of four desks set up in the room to accommodate the preround conversations. At Bob's signal, 3 or 4 teachers and support staff members go to each of the different desk clusters as preassigned by Bob. Teachers at most of the clusters represent a mix of disciplines; in a few cases, the teachers are teaching some of the same students, in a few they have none in common. The different configurations of teachers assure different subject-area and grade-level perspectives. The preround conversations are unusually short due to time constraint—only six minutes each; there are fifteen preround conversations in total, three at a time.

The preround conversations cover a lot of ground in the short time allotted. As Round veterans and colleagues who share a common language of practice and familiarity with each other's work, the teachers are focused and crisp. They share their Round sheets and review essential background on their students and the curriculum, their focus of learning, and the questions they have framed to guide observation and inquiry. They also take advantage of shared knowledge of individual students. They refer to particular students by name, citing progress or goals or strategies in relation to them and the lesson. It is a little bit like what I imagine speed dating to be—Bob signals when to switch at six minute intervals and participants quickly cycle through four groups each.

Below I give a brief synopsis of the several Teacher Rounds that I attended but in the order of the grade level they represent rather than the order in which I viewed them during the Rounds day.

Ordered by grade level, the Rounds reveal more readily whether and how different elements of instruction emphasized at UPCS support the academic development of students over time; they better illustrate the potential value of Rounds in assessing and building instructional coherence in a school in line with its planned or hoped-for trajectory of academic development for students. As it turns out, this particular Rounds day helped bring to light an area of academic literacy and practice that the teachers and principal agreed warranted more attention in the school's curriculum, as I will explain.

Kevin's 7th Grade English Class

Kevin's avuncular manner with kids is apparent even in the pre-round, as he describes their development as readers and wordsmiths. His students have just finished a stint of reading nonfiction in a literature circle format. One of their shared responsibilities "was to use their word sense" to infer meaning of a word without help from a dictionary, teacher, or peer. Students have been introduced to a number of meaning-making strategies, using new knowledge of prefixes, suffixes, and root words, applying what they know about parts of speech and practicing using context clues. In today's lesson, Kevin wants to build on this momentum, as he explains in his Round sheet: "I want to bolster their understanding of word parts and to also help them strengthen their strategies in building word knowledge." Kevin constructs the lesson in several parts: a "starter" to review strategies, group work focused on developing word sense, a collaborative short piece of fiction that incorporates their word work, and a concluding reflection on why what they have been doing is important.

Kevin's lesson incorporates several learning tools from the UPCS instructional framework: group work, writing-to-learn, and classroom talk. He frames his Round inquiry accordingly: he asks Round observers to pay attention to students' inferences and whether they are valid (writing-to-learn and classroom talk), to whether and how students help each other in solving word problems (collaboration), and to whether students explain their thinking clearly in response to questions (talking-to-learn).

During the actual Round, students begin by discussing the meaning of a series of unfamiliar words in a paragraph full of verbal mischief, created by Kevin. As Kevin has explained to them, "I wrote these purposely hard. . . . If I didn't have high expectations I wouldn't respect you." Some of the words have common suffixes; many students use these in an effort to decipher meaning, as the excerpt from my Round notes in Figure 5.1 suggests. At different points, students run up against the limits of what they know. This leads to creative meaning-making in a couple of instances—as when a student decides to simply take out the "c" in "ascend" in order to make a word that communicates the act of sending. This is a sign of students working hard to make sense of words but not always connecting context and meaning.

The postround conversation, held the next morning, focuses mainly on how students worked together, how they were making sense of unfamiliar words, whether they could explain their reasoning, whether they were persevering, and the accuracy of their inferential thinking. Meghan notes that the seventh graders enter confusion less easily than their high-school counterparts and reflects on the importance of making explicit different ways to address confusion so that students tolerate it as something they can work through. The pivotal question for the group is how to encourage students' thinking and at the same time help them to figure out the actual meaning of a word. In broader terms, the group grapples with how to create space and support for students' ideas to emerge, develop, and stand credibly on their own. Kevin muses that it might help students' thinking to add a step requiring them to answer, "How do you know [your definition] is right?" He will start the next class with some modeling along these lines.

Sarah's 7th Grade History Class

I am able to stay for only a short part of Sarah's Round in order to attend another at a different grade level and miss the postround. But what I hear and observe fits the pattern of learning for the Round day—for both students and teachers—and is echoed in the final faculty discussion. So a brief report is in order.

Sarah is intent on initiating her young charges into the world of historical thinking and discussion. During the Round, her students,

Figure 5.1   Kevin's Round: Sample Observation Notes

Round Question: Do you see students make valid inferences?	
Round Observation Notes	*Reflections/Questions*
S-S (Student-to-student interaction):	
S-A (Student A): "I know suicide and homicide have to do with murder so phobicide must have to do with killing."	Prior knowledge . . . use of suffix (cide)
S-B: "I think it means to be scared of suicide because I see the word phobicide and that means scared and I see 'cide' for suicide and that's why I think that."	Students explain their reasoning (using word knowledge)

placed strategically in small groups of four, will begin cycling through six different primary source documents from the Hebrew Bible, all connected to their study of the ancient Israelites. To facilitate the reading of what UPCS teachers commonly call a "complex" or "challenging" text, Sarah has prescribed several steps: a period of silent reading, the formation of an open-ended question by each group member, and discussion based on the open-ended questions, followed by a written response. Writing, collaboration, and questioning—three staples of UPCS instruction—act as a scaffold for the learning process. These students have prior experience answering open-ended questions in a whole group "Socratic Seminar" format; this is the first time they will try in groups what Sarah characterizes as a "miniseminar"— students are being eased into a collaborative mode of learning.

One of the documents is an excerpt from the Book of Daniel in the Old Testament of the Bible (Sarah is interested in what students will consider credible as historical information from this source). The language and syntactic structure prove daunting to the group I observe, evident as they take turns reading it. One student asks, "Do you think this story could be true? Use evidence from the story to back up your statement." The academic tenor and purpose are unmistakable! But a group member responds, "I don't understand the story." The question of how to help students pry open the meaning of this and similar texts recurs during the Round day.

Kyle's 10th Grade Geometry Class on Cell Phone Triangulation

In her preround orientation, Kyle rapidly describes her artful plan to engage her 10th grade geometry students in graphing equations and noting inequalities. She will ask students to help with a criminal investigation by identifying the likely location of the main suspect ("notoriously ruthless embezzler A-Debt") using cell phone triangulation. The students will start with three equations whose graphs form a triangle. Each vertex of the triangle marks the location of a cell phone tower; students must identify the coordinates of each, based on the city grid. Using their understanding of inequalities, students can then narrow down the "feasible region" harboring the suspect and communicate this vital information to the authorities. Finally, they must determine the approximate location of the suspect's cell phone by plotting the signal strength of each cell phone tower based on its radius in miles, which is given, and then highlighting the overlapping signal areas as part of their graphic display. As much as Kyle hopes that her students will use "two-column proofs," she emphasizes that her main focus in the lesson—and for the Round inquiry—is on student reasoning. The lesson depends on collaboration and this is an additional focus for the Round. Students will be assigned to groups of three based on Kyle's assessment of their mathematical understanding and their strengths in group problem solving.

It is 8:00 a.m. as the Round begins, and several students are finishing orange juice and cold cereal against a backdrop of student-generated geometric shapes and an explanatory poster asking, "What are proofs?" Kyle intends to start the class with a YouTube clip showing a scene from a criminal investigation TV show that explains how they locate criminals—but internet access is balky and she has to improvise ("How do they locate criminals on NCIS?"). She then gives students a handout describing cell phone tracking and triangulation. Her first question—"What are you going to do before you start the problem?"—is a familiar teacher cue to start thinking in terms of mathematical and academic literacy. One student responds, "Underline . . . stuff that's important." Kyle's instruction is more expansive—she tells students to highlight "anything that you notice"—a common starting point for engaging with a text at UPCS, intended to make a text readily accessible to any student. After several minutes with the text, a handful of students have things to offer and Kyle fields all of their ideas.

The problem having been decoded, Kyle encourages students to "jump into" it. Students respond readily, as they have known Kyle since she was their 7th grade teacher. Most start on the graphing; some work individually before comparing their graphs with others, others take the lead in illustrating. There are examples of students tapping into each other's thinking—of sharing and using each other's relevant mathematical understanding and thinking process in solving the problem. One student explains her "determination to figure this [the inequalities] out." Kyle circulates, seeks to uncover the thinking of one group by asking, "How did you get that?" and judges that another group's struggle can be productive—"I'm not telling you—you know how to figure it out." Triangles, with cell towers drawn at the vertices, and shaded areas representing the likely location of the cell phone appear on all students' work.

In postround discussion, the group agrees that all students were engaged, notwithstanding their different starting points as math learners, in trying to solve the problem. Attention then focuses intently on individual students, the support each received in the group context, and their reasoning and understanding. Student A, for example, who paid close attention to how one other student in her group explained her reasoning, confidently showed her work after Kyle checked on "whether she gets it." One of Kyle's takeaways from the Round is the question of whether and when to highlight a facilitator role for each group—someone to act as teacher—to ensure that each student's thinking is teased out and supported. Students otherwise depended on a well-developed habit of sharing work and drawing on each other's mathematical and personal strengths.

Dan's 10th Grade English Class

Kyle's students migrate to Dan's 1.5 hour English block, stepping from a world populated by cell phone towers into the politically riven world of Julius Caesar, from the precise and quantitative language of triangulation and equations into the allusive and poetic language of Shakespearean drama. Yet, in spite of this major shift in discourse, there is a striking similarity in the classes.

Dan, a veteran UPCS teacher, sets up the day's lesson to bolster students' knowledge of the main characters in *Julius Caesar*. As he notes in the preround, students have finished reading the play, but "gaps" remain in their knowledge of the characters and plot. He attributes these to the inherent challenges posed by the language of the text, its foreignness; students do not readily construct the plot or meaning, especially upon first reading. Today they will revisit the text for this purpose. In assigned groups, they will identify the source of 30 different statements made by Brutus, Caesar, Cassius, or Antony, and write what it "shows us about that character." Students will reform in character-based groups, look for patterns in the attributes of their particular character, list four principal character traits, and provide a "poignant quote" (what Dan playfully calls a "beefy nugget!") that captures the character, together with a commentary written in at least two full sentences—all on a piece of large chart paper. Finally, each student will write a character sketch in their "reader response journals." Dan's Round inquiry is fueled by concern for how well students are interpreting the Shakespearian language and using textual detail to support their characterizations. He is also interested in whether "the culture of the room fosters student engagement."

Students work actively through the Round. They divide up the work of matching quotes to characters, but the division of labor is not equal in all cases. In one instance, for example, one student finds the source of a quote and passes on the responsibility of explaining its significance to a fellow group member (referred to as Student A in my

Round note excerpts in Figure 5.2). Interestingly, this is the same student who, just prior in Kyle's class, carefully followed the work of another group member as a prelude to doing her own; she participated in her group diligently each time but also adaptively according to her strengths. Another student is not afraid to voice uncertainty in his group, questioning whether they have done right in attributing a quote to Brutus, not Caesar; it is a signal moment for the student and the group, when getting it right is more important than simply getting it done (see notes in Figure 5.2).

The posters produced by the character-based groups list four traits with supportive quotations and related commentary. A different student takes responsibility for each trait in the Cassius group. Assembling a quartet of strong words, the group brands Cassius as "greedy, overconfident, jealous, and insecure"—"He is jealous that Caesar is on top of him . . . Cassius wants the power but he can't." After brief group presentations, Dan reminds students that their one page character sketches are "in words!" and they should "smoothly incorporate two beefy nuggets [i.e., quotes]," as well as two elaborate "cumulative-style" sentences (code for sentences with a cascade of apt phrases, clarifying clauses, and choice words). He wants them to learn their own literary power as well as how to use words as evidence.

Discussion in the postround focuses intently on the question of students' misconceptions about the characters and their origin in students' readings of the text. The confusion of the group that matches Brutus to a quote from Caesar is a touchstone. But there is also some students' misconstruing of Antony's funeral oration as a

Figure 5.2 Dan's Round: Sample Observation Notes

Round Question: Are students accurately and logically using textual detail as their basis for interpretation? How do you know?	
Round Observation Notes	*Reflections/Questions*
Student A locates quote in text, then hands the piece of paper with the quote to Student B. Student B writes on the back.	Student A takes the simpler task, defers to Student B—what does Student A understand?
. . .	. . .
Students in one group attribute a quote to Brutus; it shows "ambition, patriotic, prideful"—but one student questions whether the speaker is Brutus or Caesar.	A moment of uncertainty that students honor—how do they find out whether the speaker is actually Caesar?

condemnation of Caesar. The day's lesson refocused students on the characters and the text as Dan had hoped, but it also made clear the importance of scaffolding careful and close rereading if students are to enter the Shakespearian world fully and benefit from the journey. Part of the challenge entails helping students to realize the value of rereading and revisiting the text. Dan says he "used to get a lot of pushback." Meghan mentions "slow" reading—close and careful reading—and repeated reading and writing. Students will be digging into the text again the next day.

Meghan's 12th Grade English Class

Coincidentally, Meghan's students are also encountering Shakespearian tragedy—in the form of *Hamlet*. Meghan is working out ways, in her own practice, to enable students to understand and interpret the text on their own. She is scaffolding a gradual release of responsibility by guiding them in using a repertoire of tools for comprehension and analysis, individually and in small groups. She is intentionally cultivating what she calls in the preround "college-ready behaviors"—the class is a penultimate checkpoint in the development of students as independent readers, writers, thinkers, and speakers that began when they were studying words and writing-to-learn as seventh graders in Kevin's class and that continued in classes with Sarah, Kyle, and Dan; indeed, that began the moment they stepped into the school. Meghan has a unique before-and-after perspective, having nurtured students' early development when they were seventh graders in her literacy class.

During the preround we learn that Meghan has immersed students gradually in the play during the two weeks leading up to today's class. Students have observed a slide show of the main characters, chosen one to get to know better, and performed a soliloquy by that character (a few performed for Meghan's seventh graders). The reading of each scene in the first two acts has been accompanied by an assignment—to draw a picture of events in the scene, for example, or, as in Dan's class, to list character traits with supporting evidence from the text.

Most of all, Meghan wants students confidently and constructively to engage the text, to "learn to figure out what they need to do to make sense of material on their own." Part of her strategy is to embrace confusion and complexity as norms in learning rather than as signs of incapacity; what matters is how difficulty is unwrapped and the persistent striving for meaning. She asks students to frame a question about whatever perplexes or stymies them in the reading ("What does this passage mean?"), say what they have tried to do to figure it out, and invite their peers to weigh in with their own questions or interpretations. They will do this in "tutorials," a small, supportive study group format that Meghan has conceived, again keeping in mind what will serve students well in college. Each student brings his or her puzzlement or question to the tutorial; group members honor and respond to it. The title of Meghan's Round sheet makes her intention explicit: "Shakespeare is Confusing and That's Okay: Facing Difficult Texts Head-On through Tutorials." Her two Round questions follow:

"What 'college-ready' behaviors do you see exhibited? Please include names of students."

"What do you notice about confusion levels in the classroom? Do you get the sense that they are 'too high,' 'too low,' or 'just right?' For which students does confusion tend to promote learning? For which does it seem to hinder learning?"

She is interested in all of the particulars of what happens and for whom—what specific supports or strategies different students draw on or offer in their groups—and ideas about what additional support might have helped in individual cases. In her Round inquiry she seeks to know what students are doing about what they don't know, what strengths and independence they are gaining in working with challenging and complex material. Meghan will walk from one tutorial group to another with these questions in mind, clipboard in hand.

Students come to their tutorial groups prepared with "ACT II tutorial" notebooks and at least one nagging question based on recent reading. One student at a time poses his or her question and listens to responses from three or four peers. Each question seems a genuine musing rather than academic mimicry: students venture intellectually, show willingness to expose their real thinking, search for the meaning of what they are reading—what Meghan is hoping for.

Here is an illustrative sample of questions and responses from one tutorial group:

- Student A asks, "After Hamlet sees the play, and Rosencrantz and Guildenstern leave, what is Hamlet's passage about?" One respondent says that Hamlet wants to see King Claudius's reaction—"if he flinches it reveals the truth to Hamlet. [Hamlet] wants to be sure before committing murder." Another student suggests that Hamlet is looking for "a distraction from his pain."

- Student B, who has perhaps traveled the farthest among his peers in terms of taking an active part in group discussion, is venturesome and disarming: "I see Hamlet less than a character in the play and more as a threat to Claudius. Am I totally nuts for this idea, or not?" A group member helpfully seeks clarification, "Are you trying to say that Hamlet is becoming a big enough threat so he can do something about it?" Another student offers that Hamlet is a "person who's upset about what's going on . . . he's a confused character and trying to be unconfused." A third adds reflectively, "You should fear people most who have nothing to lose," while a fourth suggests that "Hamlet's character is a threat." Students write notes in their notebooks.

- Student C asks, "Do you think the king really killed his brother? Was he really that power hungry? Think on what we learned today—is there something else behind it?" One student thinks that Claudius wants Hamlet to look upon him as a father; another sees Hamlet as searching for "why his brother would do such a thing;" a third wonders whether Hamlet "wants power, wants to become king."

Like the questions, the responses, too, seem authentic. At the same time, they tend to speculate and theorize. What they may need, in addition, is to be checked against the text, to see what ideas hold up in light of Shakespeare's subtle rendering of his characters. As in Dan's class, Meghan is trying to instill the habit of revisiting the text and to help students realize the reward, in terms of clarity, that comes from reentering its complexity.

Meghan suggests the value of returning to the text when she reports to the whole class of students what she "noticed" while listening to the tutorial sessions. She points out the clarification of the relationship between Hamlet and Polonius one student obtains by reviewing a passage. She also affirms students' musings—"we got messy with it [in order] to go deeper." She asks for students' exit slips—jottings about what they learned, what they think will happen in the play, and what they are wondering about.

The postround discussion dwells on several themes: the indications that the work Meghan did to prepare students for their study of

Hamlet helped build footholds for entering the text; demonstrations of "kids willing to admit their confusion" and their "patience," as sympathetic colearners, with each other's confusions, of students learning what to do about what they don't know, of students learning to build meaning with a measure of deliberation and care; and the importance, as in Dan's class, of getting students to say how they know when they make a statement of interpretation, of drawing on the text to substantiate and deepen understanding. Implicit throughout is the question of the trajectory of students' growth as learners ready to engage challenging material, as learners ready for post-secondary education.

What Have We Learned?

Clusters of teachers draw postround discussions to a close and the principal invites general observations and reflections on the Rounds day. Meghan begins by saying what she noticed, echoing Kyle's instruction to her class; begins, in other words, with observation. It is typical teacher and principal discourse at the school, consistent with the Rounds process and also with the classroom discourse teachers like Meghan and Kyle use to draw out students' thinking: the parallel is striking. It is a dispassionate stance, the stance of a respectful learner: to notice is to open perspective, to promote seeing rather than judgment as the pathway to understanding.

Meghan notices the creation of safe spaces for thinking, for kids to admit being confused. Kevin notes challenging lessons and material, scaffolded to enable students to make their way through. Kyle speaks to themes of collaboration and community that thread through the learning process; she mentions kids getting better at talking with each other, letting each other speak, and pulling in each other's contributions, not always in obvious ways. Ricci highlights "purposeful, meaningful conversation" and also questioning—kids asking clarification of each other's thinking and also learning to inquire in ways modeled by their teachers. Dan talks about the benefit of seeing how younger students learn to have conversations that bring ideas and meaning into focus and suggests how teachers of older students, such as himself, can learn "what it takes" from teaching the younger ones. Teachers offer examples of ways in which the learning framework of the school—processes such as writing-to-learn, clarifying talk, questioning, literacy circles, and collaboration—is being implemented so as to develop students as readers, writers, thinkers, and speakers.

The conversation attests to the values and learning theory of the school, the faithful effort to express them in practice, and a coherent learning community, with a shared and growing knowledge base and expertise, for both students and adults. The UPCS learning framework orients practice throughout the school to its purpose to form capable and persistent thinkers and to instill habits of thought and work in line with the disciplines of formal learning. The character of learning is similar from one classroom to the next: tools such as writing and talking are tied to the process of clarifying ideas and reasoning carefully; together with the curricular emphasis on challenging and meaningful problems and questions, they help open up and draw out thinking, help students develop and refine their ideas and their expression of them. But the tools only play their role in the hands of teachers attending willingly and carefully to what their students are writing, saying, and doing, individually and together, and with students increasingly committed to attending to one another. The Teacher Rounds process helps UPCS teachers maintain their attentiveness to students and to their shared vision of education.

But the Rounds Day is also revealing in ways that are not directly expressed. The school's deeply held belief in learning as both personal and social—more deeply, as communal—also comes to the fore. The reflections bespeak the teachers' commitment to a pedagogy that creates an optimal zone of learning for all of their students: one that ensures a trusted space for personal effort and inquiry; that validates and supports struggle and persistence; and that gives students tools and fosters habits to makes their effort productive and rewarding. They also tie learning intimately to communal experience. UPCS students learn in community. This would seem hard to avoid in this small school where most students are together for six years; but it is due more to a conscious effort to put core values and beliefs into practice than to school size or length of time together. Students learn to value and learn with and from each other. Put differently, students learn just as their teachers do—perhaps because of the way their teachers do—in Teacher Rounds. In this sense, Teacher Rounds at UPCS align with research which shows a strong relationship between teacher cultures built on mutual support and trust and student well-being and performance (Bryk and Schneider, 2002).

The UPCS Rounds day does more than simply highlight the trajectory of students' development as learners and elements of practice and the learning culture which help move students along over a period of years. It is a collective taking stock and assessment. The literacy theme looms large as the backbone of students' academic development. The wrap-up conversation converges on a commitment to think more about the development of students as careful and critical readers, about ways to engage them in comprehending more thoroughly and deeply a given text. This theme will focus teacher learning in grade level and disciplinary teams for the rest of the year.

For Consideration and Reflection

Rounds Day Schedule

A "Rounds Day" can be set up according to whatever logistical support a school can provide. The UPCS "Rounds Day" occurs over a period of a day and a half, the individual postround conversations and whole school wrap-up taking place the morning after a full day of Rounds. In schools where logistical concerns are more limiting, a Rounds day can instead be a Rounds week or some other variation. During a Rounds week or series of rounds weeks, a grade level team or disciplinary or interdisciplinary teams might schedule one Teacher Round each day, providing enough classroom coverage to allow 3 to 5 teachers to participate in each Round. A whole school conversation would follow after all teams finish.

Rounds Day Focus

The focus of a Rounds day is a matter of joint discernment and choice. UPCS chose to focus this particular Rounds day on the shared instructional framework that helps orient practice and learning at the school. They also wanted to mix disciplinary and grade level perspectives, thus providing an opportunity for cross-cutting conversation and cross-fertilization of practice. The teachers just as easily could have focused on grade level practice and learning, or purely disciplinary practice and learning, or emphasized one theme, such as integrating literacy development and content-area learning. They might also have simply left it up to each teacher to choose a focus that made sense to him or her. There is value in all of these approaches.

An elementary school might choose guided reading at one or more grade levels, the progression of mathematical or scientific thinking over several grades, or some other theme. Schools, in other words, can choose what makes sense in light of the development of practice and the learning of students in their particular context.

Here are questions to consider in determining the focus:

- What purpose(s) will the Rounds day serve at your school?
- Are there shared understandings or commitments regarding student learning—as in the UPCS instructional framework and emphasis on developing college-ready readers, writers, thinkers—that might serve as a basis for the Rounds day?
- Is there a specific challenge of practice that might unify the Rounds day—for instance, how to support writing development in the context of content learning?

School staff might decide that a single focus will not drive the Rounds day; but, rather, that the Rounds day will be an opportunity to generate shared questions or concerns regarding student learning and practice. There is some parallel with the UPCS example in that teachers clarified a mutual concern for students' development as critical readers as a result of the Rounds day.

Preparation and Variations

Preparation for a Rounds day (or Rounds week or Rounds month) at a school might take different paths, depending on the Rounds day purpose and teachers' prior experience with Teacher Rounds or with sharing their practice. Here are some questions to consider:

- What preparation for a Rounds day would help make it successful at a particular school? Do individual teachers or groups of teachers have prior experience with Teacher Rounds that they can share?
- What if the first Rounds day were done instead as a series of weekly Teacher Rounds, with groups of 4 to 5 teachers taking turns weekly? Who is ready to try first?
- For any teacher or group of teachers trying a Teacher Round for the first time, what support might be provided for the development of the Round sheet?
- During a given year, what if teachers were organized into Teacher Round teams—that is, organized by grade level, subject area, teaching experience, or some other principle so that they could support each other in preparing Round sheets and conducting Rounds in line with the Rounds day focus—or in line with a mutually agreed upon team focus

generated from a close examination of student learning or an interest in a particular instructional approach.

Preservice Rounds Day (or Mixed Preservice/In-Service Rounds Day)

If you are conducting a preservice program, you might similarly hold a Rounds day at a partner school, creating an opportunity for joint reflection on practice among teacher preparation students and school and university mentors (see more on Teacher Rounds and preservice learning in Appendix B).

6

Deepening Inquiry, Observation, and Reflection

The Teacher Round protocol will start teachers on a path of collaborative learning in and from practice. Thereafter, the depth and value of the learning will depend on how well group members inquire, observe, and converse reflectively. To some extent, these habits of Teacher Round learning and reflective practice can be cultivated through the process itself, as a matter of collaborative learning-by-doing. Yet it can be enormously helpful as well for Round partners to deepen understanding of what these habits mean, both conceptually and in practice and to work together to develop them. Since inquiry is the lynchpin, it comes first in the order of consideration.

The Challenge of Inquiry

In preparation for his first Teacher Round, a beginning teacher poses as a Round question whether students are "analyzing the material." For her first Teacher Round, a colleague asks whether students are "working collaboratively in their assigned groups." As part of another inquiry, a teacher intern wants to know, as a learning-centered question, whether students "are engaged." The virtue of these Round questions is that they reflect important educational concepts: the intellectual skill of analyzing; collaboration as a social learning process; and engagement as a code word for students connecting to and cogitating about subject matter. Their limitation is that they are generic and nonspecific, when something much more distinctive and aligned with the Round Teacher's learning focus is possible. What will students be doing that can be considered *analysis* or *collaboration* in this particular class? What does *engagement* mean vis-à-vis the curriculum? What would we expect to see or hear as indicators that any of these concepts were brought into living, breathing action with this particular group of students? The Round teacher and Round partners can address questions such as these during the preround orientation. In the process, the Round Teacher's assumptions about what the concepts mean in action may get teased out and given three-dimensional form, resulting in greater understanding of the teaching and learning of the day and perhaps of practice more generally and a sharper Round inquiry.

The formation of a Round inquiry is not necessarily simple, especially for a beginning teacher just learning to parse the particulars of teaching and learning: how to gain students' interest and trust and open up their minds; how to determine what equity and engagement mean in relation to particular content and curriculum goals and students; how to assess students' academic and literacy development and foster their disciplinary thinking; how to personalize support and cultivate mutual support; and perhaps how to represent democratic and community values in the classroom. Even if well-conceived in an intellectual sense, actual practice often starts as something undifferentiated and highly generalized before it becomes more analytical and comprehensive and before belief transforms in some observable way into practice. The Round inquiry therefore often starts out as something broad before it becomes incisive and penetrating.

Inquiry That Opens up Teaching and Learning

How might the generalized Round questions noted above evolve so that they lead to a clearer and deeper inquiry into the teaching and learning of the day?

What "analysis" and "working collaboratively" mean in Ricci's history class

Encouraged to elaborate and be as explicit as possible, a teacher might translate *analyzing* into something more reflective of the actual thinking entailed in relation to the subject matter, the task, and expected learning. Consider, for example, Ricci's plan for his 11th grade history students' study of the philosophies of W. E. B. Du Bois and Booker T. Washington. He has structured the day's learning so that students progress from a process of comprehending the arguments made by each thinker to advance the status of the "Negro" in society to comparing, contrasting, and then historically analyzing them. For students, the historical analysis entails situating the thinking of Du Bois and Washington in the context of their lives and times, figuring out why the two men may have thought in the way that they did, and why their thinking was different or the same from what came before or after. Ricci's Round inquiry reflects this process, asking for evidence of the learning he hopes will take place:

1. Comprehension: What evidence do you see in the small group discussion that students understand their assigned article? With what concepts or issues did they struggle?

2. Compare and Contrast: What evidence is there in the whole class discussion to show that students understand the similarities and differences in the Washington and Dubois arguments for improvement of "Negro" status in society?

3. Historical thinking: To what extent did students put the arguments in the historical context of the times, using evidence from the different documents at their disposal and their prior study? Make connections between the periods before (to give them rationale) and after these arguments, including the present? What evidence?

Implicitly, Ricci is also asking about his pedagogy—in particular the scaffolding he will use to support the development of students' historical understanding and historical thinking. Part of his pedagogy involves providing students with appropriate documents for study and preparing small group tasks and expectations. For Ricci, in this particular class, "working collaboratively" has a very specific meaning. Students will share with each other their connections, questions, and insights from reading the documents, which have been recorded in "double-entry" journals (one column for recording significant phrases and passages, the other for the student's reflection on what they put down in the first column). They will also summarize the main ideas of each thinker. If he were to add Round questions focused on this collaborative learning process, they might be: "Do all students share insights in small groups from their double-entry journals? Do group members reach agreement on what they understand to be the theories of each man and on the evidence from the documents that supports their understanding? What, if any, differences in understanding do they reconcile and how?"

What "engagement" means in Kate's Teacher Round and Holly's Teacher Round

What of the teacher thinking about *engagement*? Consider Kate's Round used as illustration in Chapter 2. In the context of her math lesson, engagement becomes initially a question of accessibility and equity: Is everyone actively at work figuring out the number of seats for different numbers of banquet tables? As the lesson progresses, the focus of engagement shifts to whether students are trying to identify a "rule," and whether they are sharing and developing their reasoning verbally with partners and in writing to the "function coordinator."

In her Teacher Round, Holly is focused on a group of Pre-K students developing number sense. Engagement for these students means something very specific in the context of her lesson. As signs of engagement, she asks Round partners to listen for evidence of students using "math talk"—*counting, comparing quantity*, and making predictions about operations (how adding 1 to a number will change the quantity).

Levels of Round Inquiry

A Round inquiry constructed so as to open up—make transparent—the learning process, in its specific context, lends itself to making focused observations that, in turn, can feed reflection and understanding of practice. Figure 6.1 suggests the general path of development of these questions, using a rubric format. In the first phase of development, there tends to be a natural concern for success in implementing plans and for general goals; questions such as "Are students analyzing the material?" and "Are students engaged?" fall in this beginning category. At the developing level, the learning process and attendant practice come into clearer focus: the teacher turns learning goals, expectations, and the structure and assumptions of teacher support into questions or directions on what to look and listen for or ask students about. In the most mature or deepening phase, as in the case of Ricci's Round on Dubois and Washington, teachers form questions which delve deeply into student learning and practice; they open up learning and practice to a wide and probing view.

Figure 6.1 Levels of Teacher Round Inquiry

	Beginning	Developing	Deepening
Typical characteristics	Articulating general concerns	Turning learning goals and practice into questions	Inquiring into learning, curriculum, equity, and practice
	Questions tend to be teacher centered, focused on broad teacher actions Questions tend to generalize the dynamic of teaching and learning Questions tend to treat learners as an undifferentiated group	More questions are learning centered, focused on particular aspects of learning appropriate to the content, learning goals, and particular learners Questions seek to uncover aspects of practice or learning, to make them more explicit and transparent	Questions focus on critical aspects of how and what different students are learning Questions seek to uncover whether and how the curriculum, lesson scaffolding, and teaching practice are providing opportunity, connection, support, and challenge for all students
Questioning goals	Unpack general questions to make the specifics of learning or practice more transparent and observable ("What, specifically, are we looking or listening for or asking about?")	Develop questions centered on learning—on what students will be thinking about and doing Develop questions to inquire whether specific practices are supporting all students	Develop questions which combine concern for learning, practice, and equity
Examples of questions	"Am I teaching the material well?" "Are students engaged?" "Are students collaborating?"	"Do students give specific examples of the challenges Atticus has to meet in *To Kill a Mockingbird* in order to defend Tom Robinson in court?" "In what instances did my questions or comments help students explain and substantiate their ideas about Atticus's challenge—how do you know?"	"What do different students identify as the legal and racial issues Atticus must consider in preparing his case? How do they use the text to show support for their views?" "Please record the connections different students make between the questions of prejudice raised in the book and their own life experience."

Developing level of Round inquiry

The primary goal for beginning teachers and teachers new to the Teacher Round process, corresponding to the developing level of Round inquiry in Figure 6.1, is to form Round questions which make the learning process and teaching practice transparent, explicit, observable, and accessible. Cocoaching, individual mentoring, or modeling—in a workshop, seminar, or teacher team format—can provide the necessary catalyst for reaching this goal. Sometimes it is helpful for a Round Teacher to have a partner in the preparation of the Round sheet, or someone in a previewer role, to ask the Round teacher to think-aloud, in metacognitive fashion, about the learning process she or he hopes to foster—to say, for example, what she or he has in mind when they use *analyze* or *collaborate* in the specific context of their lesson. It can be helpful as well to ask for a description of the learning goals and how the teacher plans to have students attain them and to work collaboratively to turn the planned learning path(s) into questions or directions on what to look, listen, or ask for. If time permits, a Round teacher may want to try out planned teaching-learning activities with peers and get peer feedback on the learning as a prelude to drafting and sharing Round questions. And it is not too late in preround conversations to clarify and elaborate questions that start out broad in scope.

Deepening level of Round inquiry

Daily practice is rife with challenge, puzzlement, and uncertainty: how to turn curriculum into pedagogy that supports and challenges every student appropriately in a zone of optimal learning, how to develop students' understanding of a difficult concept, how to grow the capacities of different students to engage complex texts or issues productively, how to make sense of and respond to different students' struggles to understand, how to account for something that works with one group of students and not another, how to create multiple pathways to common learning as a matter of equity, and a host of other concerns. The Round inquiry can draw probing attention to challenges such as these, the challenges entailed in enacting values of personalization, community, and equity and in engaging students in meaningful learning—the challenges of deep practice and student engagement.

What engaging a difficult text means in Jim's Teacher Round. If you were a Round partner in Jim's Teacher Round, you would see the veteran teacher asking his tenth grade students—some not yet fully fluent in English—to find their way into the small world of John Updike's poem, "The Great Scarf of Birds." Jim wants students to realize the power of the poem and the power of their own minds to enter it, especially if it seems daunting to them at first sight ("Show me a mind thinking!" he exhorts his students). In the course of the lesson, students will revisit the poem a number of times and in a number of ways, culminating with a letter they will write to a poetry hater that must begin with: "This poem is not as difficult as you might at first think." Jim asks Round partners to pay attention to moments of student understanding based on his theory of what will deepen his students' intellectual engagement with the poem: "Do you notice that the more students read the poem and play around with it, the deeper an understanding they develop? What evidence did you see?" He also wants participants to check student "Dear Poetry Hater" letters to look for signs of students' understanding of what the poem means and how they came to this understanding.

How understanding of floating and sinking gets constructed. As another example, consider an elementary teacher who poses the question "What theories do my students articulate about which objects will float or sink?" The question can be answered with concrete observable information, and the answers promise to provide insight on how students are making sense of floating and sinking. But there are related questions which probe the learning process further: "What happens to students' thinking when they test their theories? What preconceptions or theories are more resilient to change in the face of testing and for which students? What tests are more persuasive in the face of different theories of floating and which are not and for which students? What happens as students follow the collaborative structure for the conversation—do all students offer their concluding theories and get support for explaining how they arrived at them? Do all have opportunity and support for learning?"

How do history students learn to distinguish past from present? To offer a parallel example, take the challenge in an American history class to help students understand Lincoln's attitudes toward race. As Wineburg's (2001) research suggests, some students may quickly judge Lincoln as racist depending on the evidence they consult, their idea or experience of racism, or the extent to which they try to situate what Lincoln says in his historical context and think as historians do—think, that is, in terms of the particular audience and region of the country, the prevailing views of the time and place, and Lincoln's possible political motives, among other things. The history teacher might seek to understand how different students respond to different sources of material and whether and how their views change as they encounter each source and the complication it represents. She or he might be interested in how to construct the conversation so that students of different racial backgrounds and different attitudes toward school can view the question as a contemporary as well as historical one. The

Round inquiry centers on the question: "Do students ask about and enter, so to speak, the historical context and distinguish and compare the historical context to the contemporary one?" This might have been an approach taken by Jeremy S. in his lesson on investigating Depression-era visual images, which included an image that showed a stark contrast of experience based on race (see Chapter 3).

How to support all students in unraveling Shakespeare: When teachers work in tandem to develop their practice, a powerful coherence can build in the learning culture for students as well. Consider in this respect, as a final example, Meghan and Dan, two English teachers who appear in Chapter 5, each keen to develop the capability of their students to comprehend and learn from Shakespeare.

One of the challenges of practice confronting Meghan is how to support different students stymied by the perplexities of a difficult text. An English teacher six years into her tenure at University Park Campus School (UPCS), Meghan prepares a Round sheet for her colleagues addressing this challenge, based on her 12th grade students' study of *Hamlet*. This is Meghan's first time teaching 12th grade. Like all classes at her school, Meghan's is grouped heterogeneously and preparation for postsecondary learning is an overarching goal.

In the background section of her Round sheet, Meghan describes what she and her students have done to prepare for, comprehend, and analyze what is for most a challenging text. In the process, she identifies her own challenge, pedagogically speaking: how to scaffold students' interaction with the text so that they can grow in their ability to understand and analyze it on their own; how, in other words, to construct an optimal zone of learning for her students. She is implementing, for this purpose, a group process she has dubbed "tutorials," something akin to the kind of study group experience students might benefit from in college. This is the focal point of learning for her Teacher Round: The Round is a chance to investigate how and what students are learning through the "tutorial" experience and whether the tutorials support the development of what Meghan refers to as "college-ready" habits of thinking and collaborative learning.

For Meghan, one way to understand whether students are practicing "college-ready" habits of learning is to pay attention to how they manage the experience of confusion. On the one hand, she has patiently built up her students' tolerance of confusion in reading Shakespeare; on the other, she is helping students to develop both individual and collaborative strategies for turning confusion into comprehension. One of her Round questions asks participants to gauge how well her students are doing—and exemplifies a teacher tackling head-on a pedagogical challenge and using the Rounds process to shed light on it:

- What do you notice about confusion levels in the classroom? Do you get the sense that they are too high, too low, or just right? For which students does confusion tend to promote learning? For which does it seem to hinder learning?
- What attitudes do different students have toward their confusion? How do you know? Are they comfortable being confused? Too comfortable?
- What do particular students do to work through their own confusion or to help classmates do the same?
- Are students who are overly confused adequately supported? How so? Short of giving away answers, what else could be done to help these individuals both in the short term (I'd like them to feel that they understand the play and have some sort of handle on the language) and the long term (I'd like them to learn how to grapple with difficult texts on their own)?

Meghan's Round inquiry promises to be revealing in terms of different students' tolerance of confusion, their strategies for demystifying a text, their support for each other in a study-group format, and the development of their self-efficacy. And it was, as noted in Chapter 5.

Meghan's concerns are strikingly similar to Dan's, her colleague who teaches sophomore English. Dan's sophomores are also reading Shakespeare (*Julius Caesar*) and he wants to know which, if any, of them "struggle" with the language yet persevere in deciphering it. Both Dan and Meghan are working deliberately to foster a culture of learning in which students are undaunted by unfamiliar and complex texts and develop strategies for understanding them; and, in the effort, discover meaning as well as a sense of academic efficacy. Teacher Rounds provide an opportunity for them to share and learn from each other's efforts.

The deeper levels of inquiry suggested by these examples begin to open up a more layered view of learning and practice and the possibilities they hold, taking into greater account particular students, their particular thinking, and curriculum in its democratic and social context. Harvesting the potential of this deeper inquiry, teachers enhance practice which values all students as thinkers, which supports each in developing understanding through a process of expressing, explaining, and examining ideas, which develops academic capability, and which connects meaningfully to students' personal and social lives.

The Challenge of Round Observation

As presented in Chapter 1, observation—as a matter of noticing, attending, and relating—is a personalization skill integral to teaching; it is not a matter of evaluation or judgment. A Teacher Round provides an opportunity for teachers to practice this skill with others. At the same time, much can be done before, after, and in between Rounds.

There are several features of the Round process that engage the capacity to observe. The Round inquiry can be more or less helpful depending on how it is framed and clarified in the preround conversation. What the Round inquiry and preround explanations and clarifications lead observers to look and listen for, and sometimes to ask students about, become, so to speak, the observational lens; to the extent that they open up practice and student learning to wider view, they extend everyone's depth of field and attention to detail as observers as well.

The multiple perspectives and levels of experience represented in a Round group ramp up the group's observational power. Each Round partner has a similar task based on the Round learning focus and inquiry, yet each has a different perspective depending on experience and prior knowledge. Physically, each also can take a different vantage point during the Round, each focusing, for example, on a particular student or group of students; each, therefore, is in a position to notice any of the many details that can prove the doorway to a new understanding about a learner, the curriculum, or teaching and learning more generally. Bringing their different perspectives together, Round partners have the potential to create a fine-grained picture of teaching and learning that can be corroborated within the group and examined closely during the postround reflection. In the process, each Round partner stands to gain in her or his capacity to notice, pay attention, relate, understand, and assess—to personalize.

Observational and Interpretive Drift

We see through our own predispositions. Similarly, we tend to be reflexive—the mental equivalent to a knee-jerk reaction—before we are open and reflective. The Round process and inquiry, no matter how well-defined and focused, cannot fully counterbalance the propensity each of us has to see and interpret in a certain way, through the lens of personal experience. Neither can the Teacher Round process counteract the tendency a group might have to skew attention in one direction or another or to sidle toward one particular interpretation or one person's view rather than another's. Not least, we all bring our own prior classroom experiences, whether as students or teachers, to the Round, and these shape what we look for and how we see it.

Still, we can guard against observational and interpretive drift. To do so, it is helpful to approach observation as a matter of restraint as well as conscientiousness: restraint, so that as much as possible we give our full attention to what we see and hear rather than interpret according to our own predisposed view of what is normal or desirable; conscientiousness, especially so that we do not fall prey to the assumption that because something is familiar we already understand it. Thinking that we know what we are seeing is a slippery slope: we easily take a normative view, create a narrative in our minds of what should be happening. In so doing, we begin to distance ourselves from what—and who—are before us. It is better to approach observation innocently, as if we are seeing for the first time, respecting the action in its uniqueness; we are likely to notice more and, consequently, to bring more to postround discussion.

Maintaining Observational Integrity

The first defense against observational drift or normative thinking is adherence to the Round inquiry. Round observers strive to look, listen, and ask for what the Round teacher and Round partners have agreed upon in the preround as indications of student learning consistent with the learning focus. Even if acting with the utmost faithfulness, however, Round observers might not find the task so straightforward; after all, students often take nonlinear, personal paths of learning that do not conform to expectations. Here, then, is the corollary to the principle of respecting the Round inquiry: observers need to heed moments that do not seem consistent with learning goals and take note of them. What seems to be wayward or peripheral to an observer's eye can be the catalyst for revealing postround discussion, leading to an insight about an individual student, a teacher's pedagogical response, some aspect of the structure and content, or, just as important, a clarifying question about what happened. Such discussion, in turn, can feed the development of adaptive expertise.

Observation becomes more scrupulous also to the extent that observers strive to stay attuned and attentive to what students are actually doing and saying. Adopting a learning-centered stance in the spirit of Mann and Tolstoy, observers pay particular attention to the intellectual engagement of students with subject matter, seeking to understand, to recall Mann's words from Chapter 1, what students know, feel, and need. To this end, if the Round teacher has agreed in the preround orientation that observers may interact with students with some measure of discretion, then an observer might ask a student or group of students what it is they are working on and why or ask whether a student might explain what she or he is thinking or doing in a particular moment.

There are other strategies for maintaining observational integrity. As noted in the presentation of the Teacher Round protocol, observers might, at different moments, as suggested in the preround orientation or at their discretion, record what transpires verbatim. Two observers might focus on the same group of students, crosschecking their observations during the postround. It is helpful as well for observers to use the two-column method of observation, as illustrated in the example of Kate's Teacher's Round in Chapter 2, as a tool to separate descriptive notes from reflective comments or questions. The two-column method aligns well with the goals of postround discussion to present and discuss descriptive evidence separately from personal responses.

Some Ways to Prepare for Teacher Round Observation

Here are suggestions on how teachers, as well as teacher interns, might prepare for the observation role:

- Practice observation using videotaped segments of classroom teaching and learning. Start by focusing on different aspects of practice—for example, the teacher's questions or teacher-student verbal interactions around subject matter; the participation of students—who participates in a discussion or a project or a small group activity. Strive over time for more fine-grained observation—for example, evidence of students' ideas about subject matter, about what they are thinking; evidence of what happens to ideas in discussion, whether they are developed and substantiated, dismissed or forgotten, and by whom; and attention not only to who participates but how.

- Alternatively, practice noticing using videotape or by actually observing in a classroom. By *noticing* I mean having participants simply pay attention and note what occurs that seems significant. Compare notes and discuss the differences in what people see and hear. And, as Vivian Troen (2012), co-author of *The Power of Teacher Teams,* would remind us, act and talk as if the people in the videotape are also in the room with you.
- Practice description: practice describing what one notices. It can be a surprising challenge to decouple description from interpretation and to get used to seeing and recording what is happening. It might be instructive to try to describe 30 seconds worth of videotape or classroom activity and to compare the results with others.
- Practice observation of a whole classroom, using a seating chart to keep track of different students' moments of interaction with subject matter.
- Observe several different students, each with different academic strengths and cultural backgrounds, individually for a short period of time. Aim to describe the thinking and experience of each student in detail with supporting evidence.
- Practice using the double entry format for recording observations: the left hand column for descriptive information related to Round questions, the right hand column for questions or reflections about what you see or hear.

The Challenge of Postround Reflection

The postround reflection is an effort to draw out insight from observation and inquiry and to draw out and clarify any new questions. Ideally, the postround reflection will feed the reflective planning of the Round teacher; reinforce or broaden the knowledge and practice repertoire and adaptive expertise of all involved; and build trust, communication, commitment, and solidarity in the process.

To achieve these goals, the postround reflection, like the other parts of the Round protocol, requires a certain reflective discipline and conscientiousness. Achieving discipline in reflection can be challenging. A Teacher Round compact can act as a compass in a general sense. But more explicit norms are also needed. Recall the principles mentioned in Chapter 2:

- *Focus on practicable knowledge:* stay focused on understanding teaching-learning and developing practicable knowledge, that is, knowledge that can be applied by teachers to practice, thus building their repertoire of practice and adaptive expertise.

- *Describe rather than evaluate:* use observation notes to bring a concrete record of what happened to the conversation. Turn Round questions or directions on what to look and listen for, or ask students about, into statements of what you notice, see, hear, and find out ("I noticed," "I saw," "I heard," "I found out that. . .").
- *Ask questions which clarify rather than assume or imply judgment:* seek understanding of what the Round Teacher or other Round participants are saying, more specifically, of the teaching-learning.
- *Reflect rather than react or prescribe:* frame questions and statements, such as "what if" questions or "I wonder" statements, so as to open up deeper consideration of the teaching-learning observed during the Round and of practice more generally.

Figure 6.2   Examples of Postround Reflection Comments

Type of comment	Comments that open and sustain conversation	Comments that inhibit and close conversation
Descriptive vs. evaluative	"I *noticed* that Student A determined the equivalent of 10^3 by adding 10+10+10." "I *saw* student A calculate the area of the rectangle by putting small squares inside it and counting them up. Student B added up the squares along the edges . . ." "When you asked students in pairs, based on their reading of the documents, to take a position on whether the Framers of the Constitution could have abolished slavery, I *heard* Student A say that the language of equality was clear in the Declaration. Student B talked about how women and those without property were limited."	"Student A was not prepared to work with exponents." "Student A did not understand exponents." "Student B does not understand area." "The students did not understand the meaning of equality as Jefferson used it."
Clarifying vs. implying or prescribing	"Did any other students add rather than multiply when using exponents?" "What other students mixed perimeter and area?" "In what sense did Student A or Student B take into account historical context in determining what *equal* meant in 1776? How did they use present examples as compared to historical ones?"	"The students should have known what exponents mean." "Students should learn to multiply the length and width." "The students really missed the idea of equality you were trying to have them understand."

(Continued)

Figure 6.2 (Continued)

| Reflective and inquiring vs. evaluative and judgmental | "Did the student who added up the edges explain why he thought he was determining area? *How might we respond* in this instance to help him move from the concept of perimeter to the concept of area?"

"*I wonder if* students' historical thinking might be helped if they were to distinguish what 'equality' meant then and what it means now before debating the question of what the Framers might have done? Can we make a case for students doing this analysis in pairs?" | "There was not enough review of perimeter."

"Students need more help contrasting past and present." |

Figure 6.2 provides examples of what these principles look like in practice, contrasting postround comments that open and sustain a reflective and constructive conversation and those that inhibit or close it. Some of the words that turn what we look and listen for into what we notice and hear, and that signal a focus on what happened, on learning, and on pedagogy, are italicized. For some, these principles will feel awkward and challenging to implement. To be sure, following them does not guarantee that observations, comments, and questions will be well-received or effectively communicated or conducive to learning in and from practice. In the end, as much as they may help, neither the form nor the framing of what people say is more important than group norms that build trust, openness, and authenticity in the process; put differently, the form and framing matter insofar as they build these conditions for optimal learning among Teacher Round partners. These themes receive their due attention in the final chapter.

7

The Courage to
Learn in and
From Practice

As emphasized throughout the book, a Teacher Round is a structured process of reflection, inquiry, and collaborative learning in and from practice, conducted by and for teachers. Its founding idea is that teaching is a complex practice, and that educators need to embrace and tap into this complexity in an inquiring and collaborative way, in the context in which practice actually occurs, in order to bring to the surface and examine more closely questions and possibilities in relation to critical learning goals for all students and to develop insight and expertise. Teacher Rounds harness collaboration, observation, reflection, and inquiry as powerful agents in the process of building knowledge that can be put into practice—practicable knowledge—and in the development of a strong professional learning community with a considered and coherent approach to instruction. They support teachers in their effort to create a zone of optimal learning for all students, in working their way to a sweet spot where students individually and together develop meaningful understanding and at the same time discover their personal and collective capabilities, where the what and the who of education are joined powerfully together.

Keeping to this understanding, faithful to the Teacher Round protocol, dedicated to keeping students and their learning at the center of the process, and committed to building trust and openness, any group of teachers can start to implement and learn from Teacher Rounds. Members of a professional learning community, whether fledgling or mature, can begin to incorporate Teacher Rounds into their broader effort to develop powerful practice attuned to their students and priorities. In doing so, they not only will realize the potential of Teacher Rounds as a collaborative learning practice for themselves, they will do their part to make teaching a profession in which the development of knowledge and expertise is a continuous and collegial process. This concluding chapter highlights these broad themes: the importance, to a complex and contextual practice such as teaching, of building expertise collaboratively and of teachers working in their own zone of optimal learning; the importance, for collaboration to be effective, of openness, trust, authenticity, and courage to learn; and the importance, for public education, of a democratic approach to sharing and developing knowledge within the profession.

Developing Expertise in a Complex Practice

Chapter 1 compares the development of teaching practice which supports students in a zone of optimal learning to the art of hitting a baseball on the sweet spot of the bat. The parallel between these two disparate activities might not be obvious at first blush. Examine and compare them, however, and the shared elements of their respective practices begin to take shape. Both hitters and teachers work from a frame of reference built on past experience and knowledge; both must learn to read what is happening from moment to moment, calculate how to respond based on memory and experience, and learn from what happens; that is, both must utilize and build a certain knowledge and practice repertoire and adaptive expertise.

These basic elements of practice are not unique to baseball and teaching. Doctors, as noted in the preface, also must apply past knowledge in diagnosing and treating a particular case. When there is no clear antecedent to draw upon, then the doctor must try different assessments or treatments in an effort to find out what might be wrong and what might mitigate it. The process can be iterative as well as uncertain, a pattern that many teachers would find familiar.

Mary Oliver (1994) points out the common elements of different practices while reflecting on how the craft of poetry is learned.

Poets, she remarks, just as any worker, whether "bricklayer" or "brain surgeon," "become more proficient with study and "practice." A poem, of course, is more than the sum of its parts; it is more than the tools of the craft which knit together its unique form and meaning. But knowing the craft helps a great deal. According to Oliver, "Verbal skills *can* be learned. . . . Then, a wonderful thing happens: what is learned consciously settles, somewhere inside the chambers of the mind, where—you can count on it—it will 'remember' what it knows and will *float forth to assist in the initial writing*" (p.28). In teaching, similarly, elements of craft and prior knowledge get called up and applied in the process of planning the particular poem of learning for the day.

What differentiates teaching from many other practices, of course, is that teachers must take into account many students and their many differences, and it can seem an insurmountable task to give each student the attention each deserves. Teaching is an extraordinarily intricate interplay of broad curricular concerns, carefully planned activity, momentary adaptation, and personalized response and adjustment with a particular group of students in a particular social context. To endeavor to engage all students deeply means plunging into a world of learning, full of searching and eager minds and hearts, that is idiosyncratic, nonlinear, full of its share of uncertainty and surprise, and sometimes stumbling and messy (" . . . constructing the meaning of a story, the big themes, is a thinking, messy process," Leann writes in her Round sheet in Chapter 3). Embracing, making sense of, and learning to frame, reframe, and maneuver purposefully in this world is the heart of the vocation, the human dimension which makes teaching endlessly fascinating, challenging, and enticing.

Teacher Rounds help teachers take their bearings as they travel their own paths of learning in this complex world, each path, not unlike those of their students, with its own unexpected turns, switchbacks, and moments of bewilderment. They magnify and sharpen the focus on the dynamics of practice, bringing many eyes and ears to bear on them. In this sense, Teacher Rounds align with collaborative learning practices in other fields—the baseball player whose hitting is scrutinized by a coach and fellow players; the doctor striving to determine with colleagues in a medical round what a patient's symptoms mean; or the poet explaining a work-in-progress in a writer's workshop. In the Teacher Round process, even for veteran teachers such as Kate (Chapter 2) and Jen (Chapter 4) and their colleagues, a new understanding and iteration of practice is made possible, new seeds of expertise get planted.

Much needs to and can be learned—about students and their learning, about curriculum and planning, about student strengths and adapting and responding to particular student needs, and about how to address specific questions of practice—through the reflective process of sharing, explaining, and investigating teaching-learning in a single classroom or set of classrooms, through collaborative learning in and from practice. Greater practicable knowledge is within the grasp of teachers willing to reach out for it in a spirit of trust, openness, and collaboration.

Trust, Openness, and the Courage to Learn

As many teachers can testify, trust in schools can be elusive in spite of the best intentions and fleeting once obtained. This is especially true in cultures in which measurement and evaluation hover over venturing, inquiring, and reflecting as dominant values; and ironically true, if we believe, as so often professed, that students' learning hinges on traits such as an inquiring spirit, trying persistently in the face of a complex text or problem without certainty of results, thinking carefully and deeply, trusting the power of their own minds, and working together. Openness, too, easily slips into guardedness and defensiveness in a culture prone to oversimplifying the complex work of teaching, in particular teaching that aims to personalize, presuming that it can be routinized or systematized without narrowing down students' experience of learning. Without trust and openness, authenticity, too, will likely recede, and something more contrived and constrained will take its place.

If growth in practice requires space where open, honest, trusted and at the same time reflective and inquiring conversation is the norm, what creates it? How can we fortify teachers in opening up what feel like protective walls of isolation in their classrooms, in putting at risk their sense of vocation and identity as teachers, or in making themselves personally vulnerable? There is no simple answer to these questions. But there are guideposts, and they ask of us no less than what we often ask of students in schools. Above all, establishing a zone of optimal and authentic learning for teachers requires commitment, conviction, and courage.

In describing their Teacher Round experiences at Jacob Hiatt Elementary School, Jen and Sue remember instances of vulnerability and surprise (Chapter 4). However embarrassed or uncertain they were in the moment, they turned to their peers for support and insight; Sue actually made a verbal appeal for help during one of her Rounds. At the same time, both teachers talk about how these Teacher Round experiences deepened their own thinking, heightened the care with which they crafted their lessons, and in one good way or another infiltrated their teaching. Moreover, they both connect their experience directly to the learning of their students; in Sue's words, the students went "deeper" because she did.

Jen and Sue testify to the commitment, conviction, and courage that make the difference in whether Teacher Rounds are forced or genuinely rewarding, and whether mortifying or anxious moments are transformed into edifying and uplifting ones. Their counterparts at University Park Campus School (UPCS), where the culture of trust and openness among teachers mirrors the culture of learning they strive to create for students, demonstrate the same intrepid determination. This is not at all to say that a particular Teacher Round will not fall flat in the classroom or in the Round group, even after an earnest attempt, or that all will be transformative experiences. But, entered honestly, they will result in valued learning.

Establishing a Zone of Authentic Teacher Learning

Teacher learning has an authentic zone no less than student learning, and what teachers experience in their zone of learning can influence positively what they provide for their students. Once in the zone, as teachers and their students know, the level and quality of engagement is high. Yet, creating and sustaining a zone of powerful learning for teachers is as challenging as creating one for students. Teacher Rounds can contribute because they are centered in teacher's immediate work and context. Precisely because they are located so close to a teacher's vocational home, however, teachers may need time to feel at home with them—with the protocol, with norms of inquiry, observation, reflection, and collaborative learning, and with conversations rooted in practice, including their own. Figure 7.1 provides reminders of what can make a difference in the effort to get into the zone.

Integrity of Teachers, Integrity of the Profession

Addressing what he describes as the "inner landscape of a teacher's life," Palmer (1998) outlines the gap between educational practice and the inner integrity of teacher and students. Teachers may experience

Figure 7.1 Suggestions for Establishing a Zone of Authentic Teacher Learning

- **Make student learning the motivational heart of the Teacher Round**: take an attitude of "we're all in this together for the sake of students' learning." When students and their learning (what they are learning, who is engaged and connected, how and to what end) are the common focus of Teacher Rounds, then good and relatively unself-conscious conversation usually results.
- **Address and build norms together**: an important group norm is to acknowledge, when it arises, uncertainty in what to say or how to say it. By addressing uncertainty honestly and openly, group members signal an effort to learn how to observe and share observations together and work to establish and build trust in their norms of discussion.
- **Learn to frame reflective and constructive comments**: it may help groups to develop a common verbal repertoire or set of verbal frames for postround discussions—that is, shared ways of introducing comments which keep the group's focus on understanding student learning and practice while at the same time opening up probing and constructive avenues of thinking. For example, one can offer an alternative interpretation of what has been observed or suggest an alternative pedagogical move or structure—again for consideration, not as a prescription—by starting with, "What if . . . ?" or by simply asking, "What do you think of this approach. . . ?"
- **Strive for genuine sharing**: notwithstanding any trepidation one might have, strive to make the Round an opportunity for genuine sharing and learning rather than something forced or contrived. As principal Ricci Hall reminds teachers, by no stretch is a Teacher Round the time to bring out the fine china; we want the everyday chipped plates.
- **Make the inquiry as meaningful and authentic as possible**: what is problematic or puzzling? What is worth learning about or struggling to understand in line with the learning focus? What do you really want to or need to know more about with respect to a particular student's learning, to a whole class of students, to the subject matter, or to your own practice?
- **Be venturesome**: go to the edges of uncertainty in your thinking about a particular student or group of students and your practice in forming your inquiry.
- **Ask question such as**:
  o Are we working from concrete evidence of what happened?
  o Are we learning about student learning in this context and the practice which supports it?
  o Are we focused on something meaningful?
  o Are we keeping to the Round inquiry?
  o Are we learning about learning and practice more generally?
  o Are we generating ideas and questions for group consideration?
  o Are we in a zone of authentic learning—how do we know?
- **Make room at the end of the postround reflection to ask:** "How did we do?" especially if the Teacher Round process is at an early stage of formation in the group.
- **Be patient**: it takes time to own the process, nurture it to a state of authenticity, and make it a habitual practice in the professional culture.

a discrepancy between their own sense of integrity and their own practice as they work in tension with the logic and practice of institutional culture. They may even in some sense subjugate their deeper beliefs and convictions to their own fear of the prevailing culture of accountability and evaluation. Yet, more often than not, as most of us intuitively understand, by overprotecting our own vulnerability we also limit our own opportunity and growth. What we may not be able to see as clearly, by limiting ourselves we also, potentially, circumscribe opportunities and growth for others as well, not least our students.

Palmer suggests that for all of us to practice well we need to be well. Being well means actually being more what we are, living with greater integrity—that is, being more genuinely human, with our fears as well as hopes, strengths as well as shortcomings, uncertainties as well as convictions. Our being and our doing—put differently, who we are and what we practice—are inseparably bound together. We do best when we can be our best—when we can act genuinely, with full commitment and understanding of the nature of our work but also with acknowledgment of its uncertainties and complexities.

In the Teacher Round process, who we are, our authentic sense of self, and what we do, our daily practice, can come constructively together, provided that we work to build trust, openness, authenticity, reflectivity, and genuine collaboration. To be equal to the task, we must keep uppermost what we care most about and what we teach for—the personal and intellectual development of each and every student, the sweet spot of learning. Teacher Rounds, in this sense, are no more or less for teachers than what teaching is for students—an opportunity to create an authentic space to be and to learn.

Yet, creating and living in a space of authentic learning takes courage, the courage to learn. Round teachers such as those represented in this book show remarkable courage in their willingness to learn in and from their own practice, in their commitment to teaching. Many, such as Jen and Sue from Jacob Hiatt Elementary School and their colleagues at UPCS, see their own efforts mirrored in the open and venturesome learning of their students. Ultimately, this conjunction of professional learning and student learning is what determines the value of Teacher Rounds.

An Inherently Hopeful, Reflective, and Democratic Act

A Teacher Round respects teaching as an inherently hopeful, reflective, and democratic act, as a persistent effort to find a path that will lead each student and each group of students toward greater understanding and capability in a complex world; and, eventually, to a meaningful and fulfilling personal and civic adult life. It respects, opens up, and explores the intricacies and challenges of practice committed to developing that path of learning every day. A Teacher Round, too, is a hopeful and democratic act, based on the idea that focused learning in and from practice can broaden teachers' knowledge and adaptive expertise—can help teachers individually and collectively map out daily paths of learning for all of their students—and foster a sense of shared purpose and community.

Appendix A

Introducing Teacher Rounds: Several Examples

Chandler Elementary Community School

At the time that staff members introduced Teacher Rounds, in August 2012, Chandler Elementary Community School was in the midst of a "turnaround" process mandated by the state of Massachusetts because of low student performance. The school serves a richly diverse community in Worcester, Massachusetts. For most students, English is not a native language. Most qualify for the federal free lunch program.

The school adopted Teacher Rounds as a means of sharing and developing practice in support of student learning in critical areas, in particular mathematics. Teachers met for several August days to familiarize themselves with Teacher Rounds and to prepare to implement them. Carenza, the assistant principal who organized the professional development, was aware that some teachers were unsure and anxious about the process. She intended to demystify Teacher Rounds and hoped to foster a common commitment to the practice based on shared experience and learning. There were basically four parts to her planned introduction:

1. *Conceptual overview:* The teachers discussed their perception of Teacher Rounds, identifying benefits and concerns. They voiced their nervousness and raised questions about trust, the extent of teacher control, and feedback. At the same time, they identified the benefit of learning from each other, asking questions (about practice), and developing shared expectations. Using a jigsaw process, in which individual members from one group met with a different group to discuss a specific aspect of the process and then returned to report to their home group, the teachers digested written material on the Teacher Round protocol. They filled chart paper answering the question, "What is a Teacher Round?" and summarizing different parts of the protocol. Individually, they added sticky notes with comments and questions that would be addressed later.

2. *A shared Teacher Round experience:* Carenza then conducted a mock Teacher Round with a mathematics focus. Together, Carenza and the teachers went through the preround, Round, and postround process. Several teachers were designated observers; the rest acted as students. Following the postround, teachers talked about the process, and then they posted their comments and questions on individual sticky notes on a piece of chart paper designated for each part: preround, Round, postround.

3. *Mock Teacher Rounds:* Six teachers volunteered to prepare their own mock Teacher Rounds. In each case, they prepared a Round sheet based on a math lesson they anticipated teaching in the fall. Teachers rotated as Round partners for each mock Teacher Round. They participated in the preround and postround conversations while their colleagues acted as students during the Round itself. As each of the dry runs ended, teachers posted comments on pieces of chart paper designated for each part of the process: preround, Round, postround.

4. *Whole group debrief:* Teachers continued the collaborative process during the debrief session by examining their colleagues' comments posted on the pieces of chart paper set up for each mock Teacher Round. One group of teachers focused on preround comments, another on the Round charts, the third on the postround charts. Their goal was to summarize the experience of their colleagues in following the Teacher Round protocol.

The group focused on the preround, for example, highlighted that the Round teachers "gave clear expectations, gave observers specific things to look for, and gave background info on the class (demographics and what they had learned)." They noted that some Round teachers drew particular attention to areas of practice they "wanted help with." The teachers focused on the Round process felt that "the observers clearly knew their role," used double column observation entries, and "weren't distracting" (several teachers noted that their children accept visitors to their classrooms easily and that most welcome the attention of adults on their learning). Most valued the double column format for its intended purpose to separate evidence from commentary. Finally, the postround group noticed comments framed as "what if" or "I wonder if" by Round observers and, as well, "constructive self-reflection" by Round teachers. They noted that colleagues used evidence and "stuck to" the Round inquiry, commented on the apparent growing trust in the process, and remarked on "lots of takeaways" on the part of both Round teachers and Round partners. Commenting on the teachers' reflections, June, the principal, reminded the group that "the purpose of Rounds is to help us to refine our own practice and to think critically about what we are doing. We're starting to get past the fear factor and getting to the heart of what is important about Rounds." Carenza added that the work on Teacher Rounds continued "the construction of our collaborative community."

Intermediate level teachers (grades 3 through 6) began a series of Teacher Rounds in the fall. They chose a common focus: how to ensure rigor in the daily five—a daily set of activities incorporating reading, word work, and writing. The Teacher Rounds became benchmarks for their developing practice, grounding an ongoing conversation. As a sign of how much teachers have come to value the process, one teacher requested the chance to host a Teacher Round in another area of interest—learning math concepts in an integrated fashion, rather than in isolation, by emphasizing application of more than one concept to solve a problem or perform some other task.

Claremont Academy

Claremont Academy is a short distance away from Chandler Elementary Community School. Encompassing grades 7 through 12, the school has a population of about 450 students, many of whom speak English as a second language and most of whom qualify for the federal free or reduced lunch program.

Teacher Rounds were formally introduced to the school during a pivotal moment of rebuilding and refocusing, during a whole school professional development session in August 2012. They were identified as a practice to help build a strong professional culture dedicated to providing all students with powerful learning in support of their preparation for college. The teachers had already characterized powerful learning for themselves, with many of their ideas resonant with teaching for the sweet spot as it is described in Chapter 1. They had also begun to develop lessons exemplifying their powerful learning philosophy.

Claremont's introduction to Teacher Rounds included a number of components: a reflection by teachers on lessons they were preparing in order to meet the goal of powerful learning; an introduction to the Teacher Round protocol, including a review of a sample Round sheet; participation in Teacher Rounds conducted by veteran Round teachers; and a debrief. These steps are briefly outlined below. They formed the foundation for the first set of Teacher Rounds at the school in the fall, hosted by a group of teachers who volunteered to begin.

1. *Reflect on lesson planning*

Teachers were asked to reflect individually on the lessons they were developing to promote powerful learning with the following questions in mind:

What are 1 or 2 things that you really want to understand about your powerful lesson? What are 2 or 3 things that you would look for, listen for, or ask your students in order to know whether and how they were engaged in the powerful learning you've planned for? Try to frame these as questions to answer or as directions on what to look for, listen for, or ask students.

The teachers were then asked to share their questions or directions with a partner, explaining *why* they were important for understanding their lesson.

The whole group then discussed the close relationship between their individual reflections and partner conversations and the process of developing a Round sheet and conducting a preround orientation.

2. *Review the Teacher Round protocol and a sample Round sheet*

The teachers read, reviewed, and discussed the Teacher Round protocol using an abbreviated version similar to the one provided in Appendix C. They also reviewed a sample Round sheet.

3. *Participate in Teacher Rounds*

Every teacher was able to participate in a Teacher Round hosted by an experienced Round teacher at the nearby University Park Campus School.

4. *Debrief*

The teachers debriefed as a whole school. Conversation touched on a range of topics, similar to those that bubbled up in the debriefing session that followed the introduction of Teacher Rounds at Chandler Elementary Community School. New principal Ricci Hall sounded the final note, emphasizing the importance of keeping the "focus on kids" and promising support to allow everyone to "grow into" the Teacher Round process as a core ingredient of the learning culture of the school.

By midfall, a handful of teachers had hosted Teacher Rounds for colleagues teaching at the same grade level, working with the same students, or teaching in the same discipline. As a whole, the teachers were focused on how to engage their students in powerful learning, using tools such as writing and drawing, collaborative group work, and reading strategies. Some of the teachers have begun three-part cycles of reflection and inquiry which include colesson planning, Teacher Rounds, and close examination of students' work.

North Shore Technical High School Teacher Induction Program

At North Shore Technical High School in Middleton, Massachusetts, a group of four beginning teachers, their induction coach, the principal, and an assistant superintendent for curriculum and special education formed a small start-up group in spring 2012. They decided to integrate Teacher Rounds into the support process for beginning teachers, using the concept of powerful learning—specifically, the idea that all students can learn challenging subject matter consistent with curriculum standards, especially when they are treated as thinkers—as an organizing principle. Each teacher, two in English and two in mathematics, conducted a Teacher Round over a period of several weeks. The preround orientation occurred in the morning before school began. Coverage of classes was arranged for the participating teachers for about a period and a half so that they could participate in the Round (the actual classroom observation) and the postround reflection that followed immediately.

Appendix B

Starting at the Beginning: Preservice Teacher Rounds

From midfall to late spring, Teacher Round alerts bubble up in a steady stream of e-mail messages, often in the anxious late night hours of lesson planning. "We live in uncertain times," begins one alert announcing a lesson on *Macbeth* and the difference between fate and free will: "How better to kick off the Master of Arts in Teaching (MAT) home stretch than waking up bright and early Monday to see what Fate has in store for your future as an educator?" In another Teacher Round invitation, we are enticed to join an MAT student's 9th grade algebra class where "we have just started compound inequalities (good times, I know). If all goes to plan, we will be doing some mystery clue sets on Friday, so it should be a really fun class full of thinking, teamwork, discovery, and, of course, LEARNING!"

Teacher interns in the Clark MAT program broadcast Teacher Round messages to fellow MATs, faculty members and mentor teachers, all of whom are likely to be represented when the Teacher Round occurs. Their lighthearted tone cannot hide an understandable nervous anticipation. Most of the teacher interns feel some degree of vulnerability, especially as they approach the first of three Teacher Rounds that they will conduct over the course of a full-year internship; after all, Teacher Rounds make their practice public and transparent and much is at stake for them. At the same time, their vulnerability is shared; so are their aspirations for themselves and their students and so is their interest in knowing where they stand in their developing practice. Their Teacher Round announcements are as much a call for support as they are an invitation to be reflective partners. Many of the teacher interns will cite Teacher Rounds as the most powerful learning experience—apart from their actual day-to-day classroom experience—of their intensive one year program.

Rethinking Teacher Preparation and Practice

In 2010 the National Council for Accreditation of Teacher Education (NCATE) issued a bold report on transforming teacher education that asserted the radical importance of grounding the development of practice, in a disciplined and concerted way, more firmly in practice itself (Blue Ribbon Panel, 2010). In broad scope, the report's recommendations reflected a small but conspicuous movement in favor of more extensive, practice-based, and clinically oriented teacher preparation programs, such as residencies, already underway in the United States. Among its examples of how to closely link preparation, practice, and classroom learning, the NCATE report cites Teacher Rounds as practiced in the Clark teacher preparation program (p. 11). Teacher Rounds indeed fit hand-in-glove into a practice-based learning model in teacher preparation, as well as in teacher induction programs.

In advocating a clinical model for teacher preparation, the NCATE report implicitly acknowledges the dynamic interplay of theory, practice, and context in teaching. In their more comprehensive treatment of the question of how teachers learn, Darling-Hammond and Bransford (2005) frame the interplay in terms of the development of adaptive expertise. In their characterization, a teacher's adaptive expertise involves the ability to "apply" and "innovate" at the same time; innovation is necessary because a teacher is often confronted by unique, unexpected, or unfamiliar situations in the course of teaching-learning, sometimes from moment to moment and from one student to another (pp. 358–389). The teacher has to assess and respond constructively in these instances, to improvise so as to keep students engaged in learning. Improvising in this sense does not mean trying different things indiscriminately; it is strategic and calculated, its strategic value enhanced to the extent that it is informed by learning in, from, and about practice.

The success of a clinical model of teacher development in building the foundation of a beginning teacher's knowledge and practice repertoire and adaptive expertise may depend on how well it makes the interplay of theory, practice, and student learning (context) accessible, visible, and comprehensible. While we need to learn more about beginner teacher learning in this regard (National Research Council, 2010), Teacher Rounds, in their emphasis on focused learning in and from practice, and on attentiveness, inquiry, reflection, and collaboration as key tools in the process, have shown that they can play a significant role.

Integrating Teacher Rounds into Preservice Programs

In general, Teacher Rounds can support teacher preparation by

- thoughtfully interconnecting practice, theory, context, and the development of practice;
- illustrating and inquiring into research-based or promising practices and their implementation and adaptation in context;
- exemplifying and developing the professional habits and capabilities that make continuous learning in, from, and about practice possible—in particular attentiveness, inquiry, reflection, and collaboration;
- reinforcing any effort to understand, share, and develop practice aligned with the way of knowing of a discipline and content standards, to build pedagogical knowledge or a practice repertoire in line with disciplinary habits of mind and work as well as content understanding, to learn to personalize instruction, and to develop classrooms as communities of capable thinkers, readers, and writers; and
- preparing beginning teachers for participation in professional learning communities focused on understanding and developing practice which keeps all students in a zone of optimal and meaningful learning, leading to significant student achievement.

The following are examples of how purposes such as these are being fulfilled in several different programs, all of which derive directly from or have affinity with the Teacher Round model.

Clark University Model

Teacher Rounds have been practiced in partner schools since 1995. They punctuate the yearlong MAT program. Teacher interns learn from mentor teachers who conduct Teacher Rounds to share and demonstrate their practice and then begin a series of their own Teacher Rounds (see the program description on page 134 and the portraits of Teacher Rounds in Chapters 3 and 4). Teacher Rounds are a key practice in building the professional learning community in the school-university partnership.

University of South Carolina Model

Citing the Clark model, the University of South Carolina (USC) adopted Teacher Rounds as a collaborative learning practice in its professional development schools in 2002 (Zenger, Gilmore, & Payne, 2010; Watts and Levine, 2010). The model has been applied to connect the exemplary practice of master teachers to the learning of preservice and beginning teachers. Examining their impact, USC researchers report that preservice teachers find benefit "in observing a diversity of teaching methods, learning about a diverse group of students, and demonstrating concepts learned in their education coursework."

Teachers College at Columbia University Model

Educators at Teachers College introduced a version of Teacher Rounds in their teacher residency preparation and induction program, and there are plans to expand their use. As described in the program's bulletin, "Education Rounds are an opportunity [for Teaching residents or teacher interns] to work collectively as deliberate and thoughtful learners to examine mutually identified instruction problems . . . in their classrooms for the purpose of better understanding and improving their practice" (Bikmaz, 2012). In line with the Teacher Rounds inquiry process, Teaching residents make observations based on a question of practice developed by two of their peers teaching in different classrooms at a single host school. During a follow-up debrief session a day later, the observers share and analyze their findings. More general discussion follows on lessons learned, with specific attention to prominent program themes, such as responsive pedagogy and making learning visible. The process repeats during the yearlong residency: each teaching resident hosts two Teacher Rounds and is an observer during six others.

The "Rounds Project" at the University of Michigan

Independently, "Clinical Rounds" or the "Rounds Project" has developed in the School of Education at the University of Michigan, specifically to exemplify and guide teacher preparation students in implementing "a small set of vital teaching practices" which integrate literacy development and history learning (University of Michigan School of Education, Spring 2011). The Rounds Project is distinct from the Teacher Rounds model, however, in its focus on the direct involvement of exemplary or attending teachers, analogous to attending physicians in the medical model of training, in guiding teaching interns during their actual teaching.

Toward an Integrated Practice-Based Approach: The Example of Clark University

While Teacher Rounds can be conducted for good purpose with teacher interns under a variety of circumstances, the extent of their impact and value on a beginning teacher's development depends on how well they integrate into an overall program. In the Clark program, Teacher Rounds do not stand apart. How they are integrated is best understood in the context of the teacher preparation model. Here, as an example of what is possible, are the broad features of the model:

A Yearlong Teaching Internship in a Partner School

Akin to a residency program, teacher interns are placed with a mentor teacher in a partner school from the beginning of the school year until the end of the university academic year. The long internship allows for a structured and scaffolded immersion in teaching and in the process of examining teaching and learning in light of program values of inclusion, equity, trust, authentic and powerful learning, and learning community as well as curricular and learning goals. Closely allied, it allows for immersion in the Teacher Round process.

A Cohort Experience

Teacher interns are assigned to cohort groups of at least 4 to 5 participants in partner schools. Teacher Rounds integrate readily into the cohort model. They provide opportunities for interns to share and support practice within their specific school contexts and cultures. The Teacher Rounds are grounded in disciplinary learning, but often interns from more than one discipline attend a Round together. Just as often, the interns from one partner school attend the Teacher Rounds of interns from another in order to learn from the different contexts and their shared questions or practices; the schools are in close proximity, serving students from the same large urban neighborhood.

A Collaborative Learning Culture and Community of Practice

Teacher interns conduct Teacher Rounds in a culture that supports them. Teacher Rounds have become a familiar and, in some cases, culturally ingrained practice in the partner schools; each teacher intern has a mentor teacher and university mentor who usually participate in them. Teacher interns alone conduct dozens of Teacher Rounds each year in each of the partner schools—three each, one in the fall and two in the spring. Each teacher intern attends at least five other Teacher Rounds; most usually attend more. This Teacher Rounds culture, of course, did not always exist. The teacher interns were among the first to practice Teacher Rounds in the partner schools; they were agents of change, modest ones, in their host schools' professional cultures.

Dedicated Core of University and Partner School Faculty

Consistent with recent recommendations for teacher preparation made by NCATE (Blue Ribbon Panel, 2010), and historical calls for faculty with special expertise in teacher education (Conant, 1963; Levine, 2006), the program is staffed by "professors of practice" and mentor teachers with a dedicated commitment to the partner schools and the program. One or two "teacher fellows"—exemplary teachers with release time to work in the program as well as in their partner schools for an academic year—also play an integral role. The professors of practice work in partner schools regularly, usually know and work collegially with mentor teachers on questions of curriculum and practice, and have depth of knowledge about the school setting—and to some extent the urban community context—to bring to the process as well. Typically, two professors of practice attend each teacher intern's Teacher Round.

A Common Framework for Teaching and Learning

Finally, a set of overarching principles and concerns about teaching and learning frame Teacher Rounds in the program. All commit to practice that is inclusive, equitable, authentic, meaningful, personalized, and powerful—powerful in the sense that it helps all students realize individually and together their capability as learners to develop understanding and meet curricular expectations; practice, in other words, that aims for the sweet spot of teaching and learning. In developing their practice within this framework, teacher interns must confront the question of what it means to think, inquire, and learn in particular disciplines, of how to represent disciplinary learning in an engaging, developmentally appropriate, and personally connective and meaningful way, and of how to fulfill corresponding curriculum standards. They address companion questions of how literacy development and disciplinary learning weave together and how to assess and support students in their development as readers, writers, and speakers.

A Progression of Teacher Round Learning

The general progression of Teacher Round learning in the year-long Clark program occurs in three basic stages. In reality, the stages are not so much separate as they are shifts in emphasis leading to a more comprehensive engagement with teaching and learning over time. To some extent, the shifts in emphasis may be viewed as following a more general trajectory of beginning teacher development toward greater fluency in and command of practice that engages, challenges, and supports all learners in meaningful learning. Teacher Rounds can help beginning teachers meet several of the challenges typically encountered along this path, such as

- progressing from an undifferentiated and generalized view of practice towards a more multidimensional and analytic view,
- broadening from a teacher-centered focus concerned with teacher presence and authority to a focus on practice and student learning,
- shifting attention from classroom organizational issues to questions of instruction and learning,
- learning to attend to and address individual students and their learning as an integral part of the process of planning daily curriculum and instruction and enacting equity in practice,

- taking an increasingly inquiring and reflective stance vis-à-vis one's own practice, and
- integrating the knowledge and practice repertoire and adaptive expertise.

Stage 1: Teacher Rounds open the door to the study of practice (summer and early fall)

Most teacher interns learn first about Teacher Rounds by experiencing them. Partner school teachers conduct and model Teacher Rounds for many interns during a summer academy for partner school students. In early fall, teacher interns attend Teacher Rounds closely tied to courses in disciplinary learning; in some cases, the Teacher Rounds occur in a short daily or weekly series, with the host teacher's class serving as an abbreviated case study of practice and disciplinary learning.

Stage 2: Teacher Rounds support the development of personal practice (middle and late fall)

By the end of the fall, each teacher intern will have hosted a Teacher Round and attended at least two peer Teacher Rounds. Interns are supported in their preparation in their cohort group's practice seminar and individually by their university and teacher mentors.

Teacher interns write a reflection on their own Teacher Rounds and on selected ones that they attend. They also review videotape of their own Teacher Round and prepare edited segments for a discussion with peers in their practice seminar, following a protocol.

Framing the Round inquiry is often the biggest challenge for interns at this stage. Interns interested in whether students are *collaborating* or *engaged*, for instance, may be masking other concerns. "Are they engaged?" may mean "Are they acting in a positive manner?" Interns have an understandably heightened concern for whether their students are interested or disengaged, responsive or resistant, respectful or otherwise; and, closely related, concern for their own presence, authority, respect, and efficacy. For many interns, at the time of their first Round, the most pressing question is whether they have the eyes, ears, and respect of their students.

Stage 3: Teacher Rounds build habits of reflection, inquiry, and collaboration

Teacher interns host their second Teacher Rounds soon after the turn of the calendar year, when they are 10 to 14 weeks into their teaching; their third series of Teacher Rounds occurs in the vicinity of 15 to 20 weeks into their teaching. This spacing gives teacher interns an opportunity to grow into the Teacher Round process. In this respect, Teacher Rounds become a series of reference points for their development as reflective practitioners and collaborative learners. Their Teacher Round videotapes and reflections serve as several of many important artifacts they will use to illustrate and analyze the growth of their practice and of their students' learning at the end of their program. Rounds conducted by teacher interns account for well over 100 of the many Teacher Rounds which occur in partner schools over the course of the year.

Appendix C

The Teacher Round Protocol (Sample Short Version)

Important Notes on Teacher Rounds

*A Teacher Round is about learning in and from practice. It is framed by the Round teacher.

*Specifically, a Teacher Round is about understanding student learning in classrooms and the practice that supports it. It is not evaluative.

*A Teacher Round is a collaborative process—a way to bring a number of eyes and ears to the task of learning what students are thinking and doing and what is engaging them.

*Round participants are reflective partners.

Part 1 of the Round Protocol: Preparing the Round Sheet

The Background (What, Who, and Why)

Essential questions for the Round teacher are: What do my Teacher Round partners need to know in order to understand what I have planned and why it makes sense—why it will support powerful learning—for these students at this moment? What do they need to know in order to understand what students will be thinking about and doing?

The Learning Focus

A Teacher Round ultimately turns on the question of student learning and how it relates to teaching practice. In the learning focus section the Round teacher explains the student learning planned for the day. The Round teacher also identifies the focus of professional learning for the Round.

Here are several questions to consider in developing the Round learning focus:

- Learning centered: On what learning goals am I centrally focused in this lesson? What specifically is the process of learning that students will be engaged in? What can members of the Round group expect to see or hear to indicate that students are engaged in powerful learning in line with the learning goals? To what should they pay attention in students' learning?
- Practice centered: What in particular about the teaching-learning am I trying to learn about or understand better with my Teacher Round partners? Is there some aspect of practice effectiveness I want to understand—what would help me to understand it?

The Round Inquiry

Generally, developing the Round inquiry means turning the Round learning focus into a set of questions or directions on the evidence to look, listen, or ask for in order to understand the teaching and learning.

What are 1 or 2 things that you really want to understand about your lesson? What are 2 or 3 things that you would look for, listen for, or ask your students in order to know whether and how they were engaged in the learning you've planned for?

Part 2 of the Teacher Round Protocol: The Preround Orientation

The preround orientation has three basic goals:

- To inform Round participants about the teaching-learning
- To ensure that Round participants understand the context of the Round, including any relevant perspective of the Round teacher on curriculum, student learning, and practice
- To prepare Round participants for their role as co-observers and co-inquirers

Round participants should leave the preround orientation with an understanding of the classroom context, in particular students' understanding of subject matter and development as academic learners, the planned teaching and learning and its importance, and with a clear idea of what to look and listen for and try to understand as a co-observer and co-inquirer.

The preround typically follows these steps:

1. Participants read the Round sheet.

2. The Round teacher highlights key points in each section and elaborates as needed. The Round group reviews the Round inquiry closely—what to look and listen for and try to understand—and clarifies it as needed. Round partners ask questions or make comments to ensure understanding.

3. The Round teacher explains the subject matter of the Round and engages participants briefly in learning it in order to give them a firsthand experience of what students will be doing, as appropriate.

4. The Round teacher indicates whether, how, and when Round participants may interact with students and where participants might position themselves physically in the room.

Part 3 of the Teacher Round Protocol: The Round

The Round is the actual classroom lesson. The following are sample notes from a middle school mathematics Teacher Round, using a two column format—one column with detail of what happened and the other with reflections and questions. Notes are not always this detailed or neat! This level of detail is invariably helpful when it can be achieved—these notes are a rich resource for the postround reflection.

Kate's Round question: What indications are there that students are thinking algebraically, in terms of a function rather than counting?

Observation Notes	Reflections/Questions
T (Teacher): "Find the # of seats for 3, 4, and 5 tables then do a 'jump' to 10. No talking—silent thinking time right now."	The "jump" encourages algebraic thinking
S-A (Student A): Uses chart paper and draws individual tables. Explains: "For every single [added] table add 2 more people—4, 6, 8, 10, 12, jump 22. This is how I figured out how to fill in the blanks [in his table]."	Is he adding in his head or using a "rule?"
Teacher asks whole class for "different methods" of figuring out	Explain "methods"; everyone has some method—everyone is included; makes thinking visible
S-B: "[I] counted around the edges [of the tables]. . .found the perimeter of tables which was 12. For 5 [tables], 5×2 + 2."	Is there any relationship between "adding" around the perimeter and determining a functional relationship?
T: "Figure out how many people for 100 tables. Write a letter about how to find the number of people at any given # of tables. See if you can include 'a rule.'" [silent thinking time]	Writing their thinking about a rule (work out functional relationship)
S-C: 100 tables [will seat] 220 people. T: "Let me see if I understand. . .It makes sense to me. . .Does it make sense? Why not? Think about it."	She uses multiplication (if 10 tables = 22, then 100 = 10× 22 or 220)? Ask for more explanation of her thinking? What if she compares her thinking to others?
S-D offers a "rule:" 4 (seats) × n (number of tables) minus # of "gaps" [the edges of tables that are together] × 2...	Example of reasoning that shows understanding of a functional relationship

Part 4 of the Teacher Round Protocol: The Postround Reflection

Stay focused on understanding teaching-learning and developing practicable knowledge, that is, knowledge that can be applied to practice.

Key supportive principles include:

- *Describe rather than evaluate:* use observation notes to bring a concrete record of what happened to the conversation.
- *Ask questions which clarify rather than assume or imply judgment:* seek understanding of what the Round teacher or other Round participants are saying, more specifically, of the teaching-learning.
- *Reflect rather than react or prescribe:* frame questions and statements, such as "what if" questions or "I wonder" statements, so as to open up deeper consideration of the teaching-learning observed during the Round and of practice more generally.

Three general phases of the postround reflection:

1. First thoughts: the Round teacher's initial reflection and participants' response

2. Inquiry: sharing and discussing observations based on the Round questions (describe, clarify, reflect)

3. Final reflection: what's new, what if, what next, what's left, and how did we do

4. Final thoughts: The group wraps up by reflecting on what they have learned and the implications for teaching and learning, asking some or all of the following questions:

   o *What's new?* What have we learned, what are our takeaways? The "What's new?" question opens the door for summarizing specific ideas about curriculum and practice or specific insights about teaching-learning that the Teacher Round has caused participants to newly consider or revisit.

   o *What if?* What might we have done differently and why? The "What if?" question spurs thinking about alternative possibilities for engaging and supporting students in line with learning goals and the Round inquiry. This is usually the most challenging terrain of the postround conversation. The key question is how to suggest an alternative that makes sense in light of shared evidence of what happened and the learning goals; that is, to build a plausible case for an alternative that might in some way support one or more students in learning for everyone to consider thoughtfully and respectfully. This approach helps keep the focus on teaching-learning and not the Round Teacher. It is a good idea to provide the Round teacher with the first opportunity to pose a "What if?" question.

o *What next?* What might we try next in order to support these students' learning and why? The Round teacher typically sketches plans for the following day(s) in light of more long-term goals and knowledge of how students are developing academically and discusses what modifications, if any, she or he might make based on the Round experience. Round participants clarify, comment, or suggest.

o *What's left?* What old or new questions about curriculum, teaching, and learning are we pondering and how might we address them?

o *How did we do?* Participants reflect on any or all of the following: how well they did in observing, sharing observations, meeting the goals of the Round inquiry, discussing and learning about practice together during the postround reflection, and fulfilling other group norms.

References

Bikmaz, F. (Spring 2012). Exploring teaching practice through education rounds. *Teaching Residents at Teachers College Bulletin, 2*(3).

Blue Ribbon Panel. (2010). *Transforming teacher education through clinical practice: A national strategy to prepare effective teachers.* Washington, DC: NCATE. Retrieved from http://www.ncate.org/LinkClick.aspx?filetick et=zzeiB10oqPk%3D&tabid=715

Bryk, A., & Schneider, B. (2002). *Trust in schools: A core resource for improvement.* New York, NY: Russell Sage Foundation.

Carroll, Thomas G., Fulton, K., & Doerr, H., Eds. (June 2010). *Team up for 21st century teaching and learning: What research and practice reveal about professional learning.* National Commission on Teaching and America's Future. Retrieved from http://nctaf.org/wp-content/uploads/2012/01/TeamUp-CE-Web.pdf

City, E. A., Elmore, R. F., Fiarman, S. E., & Teitel, L. (2009). *Instructional rounds.* Cambridge, MA: Harvard Education Press.

Cohen, David K. (2011). *Teaching and its predicaments.* Cambridge, MA: Harvard University Press.

Conant, J. (1963). *The education of American teachers.* New York, NY: McGraw Hill.

Cremin, L. (1957). *The republic and the school: Horace Mann on the education of free men.* New York, NY: Teachers College Press.

Darling-Hammond, L., & Bransford, J. (Eds.). (2005). *Preparing teachers for a changing world: What teachers should learn and be able to do.* San Francisco, CA: Jossey-Bass.

Delpit, L. (2012). *"Multiplication is for white people": Raising expectations for other people's children.* New York, NY: The New Press.

DelPrete, T. (1990). *The Anna Maria College-Calvin Coolidge Professional Development School Guidebook. ERIC Digest.* Retrieved from ERIC database (ED349266).

Del Prete, T. (1997). The "rounds" model of professional development. *From the Inside, 1*(1), 12–13.

Del Prete, T. (2010). *Improving the odds: Developing powerful teaching practice and a culture of learning in urban high schools.* New York, NY: Teachers College Press.

Dewey, John (1938). *Experience and education.* New York, NY: Macmillan.

The Education Trust. (November 1, 2005). *The power to change: High schools that help all students achieve.* Washington, DC: Author. Retrieved from http://www.edtrust.org/dc/publication/the-power-to-change-high-schools-that-help-all-students-achieve

Elmore, Richard F. (2004). *School reform from the inside out: Policy, practice, and performance.* Cambridge, MA: Harvard Education Press.

Fullan, M. (2007). *The new meaning of educational change.* (4th ed.). New York, NY: Teachers College Press.

Hargreaves, A. (2010). Presentism, individualism, and conservatism: The legacy of Dan Lortie's *Schoolteacher: A sociological study. Curriculum Inquiry, 40*: 143–154.

Learning Forward: The international nonprofit association of learning educators (2012). Retrieved from http://www.learningforward.org/standards/learning-communities

Levine, A. (September, 2006). *Educating school teachers.* The Education Schools Project. Retrieved from www.edschools.org/pdf/Educating_Teachers_Report.pdf

Lortie, D. (1975). *Schoolteacher: A sociological study.* Chicago, IL: University of Chicago Press.

McDonald, J. P., Mohr, N., Dichter, A., & McDonald, E. C. (2003). *The power of protocols: An educator's guide to better practice.* New York, NY: Teachers College Press.

McLaughlin, M. W., & Talbert, J. E. (2001). *Professional communities and the work of high school teaching.* Chicago, IL: University of Chicago Press.

Merton, T. (1958). *Thoughts in solitude.* New York, NY: Farrar, Straus and Giroux.

National Association for the Education of Young Children (September 2001). A conversation with Vivian Gussin Paley, *Young Children,* 91. Retrieved from www.naeyc.org/content/conversation-vivian-gussin-paley

National Research Council (2010). *Preparing teachers: Building evidence for sound policy.* Committee on the Study of Teacher Preparation Programs in the United States, Center for Education. Division of Behavioral and Social Sciences and Education. Washington, DC: The National Academies Press.

Oliver, Mary. (1994). *A poetry handbook: A prose guide to understanding and writing poetry.* New York, NY: Harcourt.

Oliver, M. (2003). *Owls and other fantasies: Poems and essays.* Boston, MA: Beacon Press.

Oliver, M. (2008). *Red bird.* Boston, MA: Beacon Press.

Palmer, P. (1998). *The courage to teach: Exploring the inner landscape of a teacher's life.* San Francisco, CA: Jossey-Bass.

Schon, Donald A. (1983). *The reflective practitioner: How professionals think in action.* New York, NY: Basic Books.

Shulman, L. (2004). *The wisdom of practice: Essays on teaching, learning, and learning to teach.* San Francisco, CA: Jossey-Bass.

Troen, V., & Boles, K. C. (2012). *The power of teacher teams: With cases, analyses, and strategies for success.* Thousand Oaks, CA: Corwin.

University of Michigan School of Education. (Spring 2011). *The whole is greater than the sum of its parts.* Retrieved from http://www.soe.umich .edu/files/rounds_story.pdf

U.S. Department of Education. (August 15, 2005). *The Education Innovator #30.* Washington, DC: Author. Retrieved from http://www2.ed.gov/ news/newsletters/innovator/2005/0815.html.

Watts, E., &Levine. M. (November 2010). *Partnerships, practices, and policies to support clinically based teacher preparation: Selected examples.* NCATE. Retrieved from http://www.ncate.org/LinkClick.aspx?fileticket=rMrsfj Z2vZY%3D&tabid=715.

Wineburg, S. (2001). *Historical thinking and other unnatural acts: Charting the future of teaching the past.* Philadelphia, PA: Temple University Press.

Zenger, J., Gilmore, J., & Payne, J. (2010). *Well rounded teachers: The efficacy of rounds in teacher education.* PowerPoint presentation. Retrieved from http://tqp.ed.sc.edu/pathpresentations.htm

Index

Note: In page references, f indicates figures.

CORWIN

A SAGE Company

The Corwin logo—a raven striding across an open book—represents the union of courage and learning. Corwin is committed to improving education for all learners by publishing books and other professional development resources for those serving the field of PreK–12 education. By providing practical, hands-on materials, Corwin continues to carry out the promise of its motto: **"Helping Educators Do Their Work Better."**